Reader's Digest
Pathfinders

Birds

A Reader's Digest Pathfinder

Reader's Digest Children's Books are published by
Reader's Digest Children's Publishing, Inc.
Reader's Digest Road, Pleasantville, NY, 10570-7000, U.S.A.

Conceived and produced by Weldon Owen Pty Limited
59 Victoria Street, McMahons Point, NSW, 2060, Australia
A member of the Weldon Owen Group of Companies
Sydney • San Francisco • Auckland • London

© 2000 Weldon Owen Inc.

READER'S DIGEST CHILDREN'S PUBLISHING, INC.
Senior Project Editors: Sherry Gerstein, Beverly Larson, Lawrence T. Lorimer
Editor: Dina Rubin
Associate Editor: Lori Froeb
Project Creative Director: Candy Warren
Art Director: Fredric Winkowski
Production Coordinator: Debbie Gagnon
Director of Sales and Marketing: Rosanne McManus

WELDON OWEN PUBLISHING
Chief Executive Officer: John Owen
President: Terry Newell
Publisher: Sheena Coupe
Associate Publisher: Lynn Humphries
Art Director: Sue Burk
Consultant, Design Concept, and Cover Design: John Bull
Design Concept: Clare Forte, Robyn Latimer
Editorial Assistants: Sarah Anderson, Tracey Jackson
Production Manager: Caroline Webber
Vice President International Sales: Stuart Laurence

Author: Edward S. Brinkley
Consultants: Kevin J. McGowan, Noble Proctor
Project Editor: Joanne Holliman
Designer: Cliff Watt
Picture Researcher: Annette Crueger

Illustrators: Jane Beatson, Dan Cole/Wildlife Art Ltd,
Barry Croucher/Wildlife Art Ltd, Christer Eriksson, Lloyd Foye, Gino Hasler,
Rob Mancini, John Richards, Peter Scott/Wildlife Art Ltd, Chris Stead

Library of Congress Cataloging-in-Publication Data

Brinkley, Edward.
Birds / [author, Edward Brinkley ; illustrators, Dan Cole...et al.].
p. cm. — (Reader's Digest pathfinders)
Summary: Text, illustrations, and activities explore various aspects of the world of birds,
including their physical structure, habitats, and behavior.
ISBN 1-57584-376-5 (trade : hc) — ISBN 1-57584-382-X (lib.ed) —
ISBN 0-7944-0002-7 (paperback edition)
1. Birds—Juvenile literature. [1. Birds.] I. Cole, Dan, ill. II. Title. III. Series.
QL676.2.B75   2000   598—dc21   99-087130

Color Reproduction by Colourscan Co Pte Ltd
Printed by Tien Wah Press Pte Ltd
Printed in Singapore

Reader's Digest Children's Books is a trademark and Reader's Digest
is a registered trademark of The Reader's Digest Association, Inc.

A WELDON OWEN PRODUCTION

Reader's Digest
Pathfinders

Birds

Reader's Digest Children's Books™

Pleasantville, New York • Montréal, Québec

Contents

What Is a Bird? 6

The Way Birds Act 24

Where Birds Live 42

Pick Your Path!

PREPARE FOR TAKEOFF on a flight of discovery through the world of *Birds*. Start at the beginning and learn about the physical characteristics of birds. Or, if you're interested in the colors of birds' feathers, jump right into "Brilliant Plumage" and move through the book from there.

You'll find plenty of other discovery paths to choose from in the special features sections. Read about discoveries by birdwatchers in "Inside Story," or get creative with "Hands On" activities. Delve into words with "Word Builders," or amaze your friends with fascinating facts from "That's Amazing!" You can choose a new path with every reading—READER'S DIGEST PATHFINDERS will take you wherever *you* want to go.

INSIDE STORY
The Champions of Birds

Imagine yourself standing in the middle of a rain forest, in the still darkness of night, recording the sounds of nocturnal birds. Find out how raising goslings won a zoologist a Nobel Prize. Trek through a blizzard and experience the excitement of discovering a rookery of Emperor Penguins. INSIDE STORY introduces you to the men and women who have made studying and protecting birds their life's work. Read these people's stories, and you'll be inspired to observe and care for birds yourself.

HANDS ON
Create and Make

Jump up and down and see how fast you can make your pulse race. Is it as fast as a hummingbird's? Use a plastic milk carton to make a bird feeder. With water and some plaster of paris, start your own collection of bird footprints. HANDS ON features experiments, projects, and creative activities that will teach you more about the world of birds.

Word Builders
What a strange word! What does it mean? Where did it come from? Find out by reading *Word Builders*.

That's Amazing!
Awesome facts, amazing records, fascinating figures— you'll find them all in *That's Amazing!*

Pathfinder
Use the *Pathfinder* section to find your way from one subject to another. It's all up to you.

Ready! Set!
Start exploring!

What Is a Bird?

ABOUT SIX BILLION people live on Earth. That's a lot. But did you know that more than 100 billion birds live on our planet as well? Most of these birds can fly, but some can also swim, and others can run faster than a horse. Birds have evolved in amazing ways so that they can survive in different climates and environments all over the world. Turn the page and start to discover what makes birds unique in the animal world.

Rufous Motmot
(American rain forests)

Desert Wheatear
(Eurasian deserts)

Goliath Heron
(African waterways)

Plains Wanderer
(Australian grasslands)

Goldcrest
(European woods)

A World of Birds

IMAGINE IF SOME of us were the size of coffee cups and others were taller than houses. That's how it is with birds. The Bee Hummingbird is smaller than a moth, and the Ostrich is taller than a basketball player. In between these extremes are more than 9,000 unique bird species.

When birds began to fly millions of years ago, they settled in different places on all the continents of the world. They adapted to life in various habitats, including deserts, rain forests, grasslands, and even out at sea. In these places they found different kinds of food to eat and made different nests from the materials available. Each species had to adapt to its surroundings, or else face extinction.

The same needs for adapting exist today. The Desert Wheatear, for example, keeps its eggs from getting too hot in the daytime or too cold at night by nesting in burrows left by desert mice or other rodents. The Goldcrest has short, rounded wings—perfect for weaving through the trees in the woods where it lives. The Goliath Heron, on the other hand, lives near water. It has legs like stilts for wading into the water, and a bill the shape of a dagger for spearing fish. The Plains Wanderer seldom flies because it doesn't need to. It has evolved in color and habits so that it can hide from predators among the grass of its homeland. Even brightly colored birds often blend into their surroundings. The Rufous Motmot of South America is almost invisible to predators in its tropical rain-forest habitat.

Bird Habitats of the World

- Cities
- Woodlands
- Rain forests
- Grasslands
- Mountains
- Hot deserts
- Polar regions

That's Amazing!

• The Ostrich of Africa is as heavy as two adult humans. It can weigh up to 300 pounds (136 kg).
• A newly hatched Bee Hummingbird chick of Cuba weighs about as much as a fingernail clipping. Its weight is less than a tenth of an ounce (2 g).

Pathfinder

• In adapting to a habitat, some birds have developed special feather colors. Go to pages 16–17.
• Does the food in a habitat have an effect on the way a bird has adapted? Turn to pages 34–35.
• Some habitats, such as forests, are home to a large variety of bird species. How do so many different species live in a single habitat? See pages 52–55.

AGAINST ALL ODDS

We see birds in the cities and the suburbs, on farmlands and the open plains, in forests, and on the beaches. But some birds live in places where conditions are so tough that even humans find it hard to survive. How do they exist?

KEEPING THEIR COOL

Most shorebirds lay their eggs in a shallow scrape on the ground. But in the desert climate along the Persian Gulf, eggs would roast. The Crab Plovers that live there dig deep holes into sand dunes along the shore and lay their eggs in the holes. The sand is moist and cool, so the eggs are protected from the hot sun.

BUNDLING UP

The thickset Adélie Penguin is well adapted for polar conditions. From a young age, these penguins grow dense, short, furlike feathers that provide protection from icy weather.

FLYING HIGH

Birds survive even in the highest of all mountains, the Himalayas. The Lammergeier has long, broad wings that enable it to glide easily in thin air for hours in search of food.

WHAT A SCOOP!

The Greater Flamingo lives in shallow lakes and coastal regions in America, Africa, and Asia. With its long legs and neck, it is perfectly adapted to its environment. When it feeds, the Flamingo bends forward, turns its head upside down, and drags its hooked bill through the water. It scoops up mud and water containing small shellfish, insects, single-celled animals, and algae in its upper jaw, which is lined with a row of slits. The bird then closes its bill and uses its lower jaw and tongue to pump the muddy water out through the slits. The food particles remain, ready to be eaten.

INSIDE STORY

To the Rescue

In 1951, a team from the American Museum of Natural History went to the islands of Bermuda off the North American coast to search for the Cahow, a bird described in the writings of early European settlers. David Wingate, a 16-year-old Bermudian, joined the searchers. The museum expedition discovered a small and endangered colony of birds. Many ornithologists think this bird is the mysterious Cahow, but they gave it a new name, the Bermuda Petrel. David Wingate was inspired by the search and became a bird specialist. He has made it his life's work to protect and study the rare petrels. Thanks to his devotion to his task, there are now about 200 petrels in the colony.

The Early Birds

YOU WOULDN'T PUT out a bird feeder if you thought it might attract a ferocious dinosaur like *Tyrannosaurus rex*. But every time you pour seed into a feeder, you could be providing a meal for one of its relatives. Scientists believe that the earliest known bird, *Archaeopteryx*, was related to the theropods, the group of dinosaurs that includes *Tyrannosaurus*. The feet of *Tyrannosaurus* and its smaller dinosaur relatives are surprisingly similar to chicken feet.

Scientists are still trying to work out exactly where birds came from. To do this, they compare the fossils of birds that lived millions of years ago with today's birds. *Archaeopteryx* dates from the Jurassic period, 208 to 144 million years ago. Bird fossils have also been discovered from the Cretaceous period—144 to 65 million years ago. These birds were more like the birds we see today. The most famous finds were *Hesperornis* and *Ichthyornis*. *Hesperornis* couldn't fly, but swam underwater after fishes, like a cormorant. *Ichthyornis* was probably a strong flyer. Built like a tern, it probably flew over the water and dived for fishes—just like today's terns.

AN EVOLUTIONARY FLIGHT

Only birds have feathers, and feathers enable most birds to be skilled flyers. No one knows what creature had the first feathers—perhaps some theropod dinosaur. *Archaeopteryx* is the first animal known to have feathers. But over millions of years, a huge variety of birds has evolved.

INSIDE STORY
Following the Past

Charles Darwin (1809–82) was an English naturalist whose theory of natural selection explained how different animal and plant species evolved. He suggested that species with features that helped them to survive within their habitat ate better and reproduced more effectively. For example, in the Galápagos Islands off the coast of South America, he noted many species of finches. He speculated that all the finches came from a single ancestor, and those that had evolved to suit the habitats had survived. So, in an area where there were plenty of seeds, finches with strong seed-cracking bills increased while finches with different bill shapes had to find food elsewhere or face extinction.

Ichthyornis

Reptilian theropod dinosaur

Archaeopteryx

UNEARTHING DELIGHTS

Imagine the thrill for ornithologists in 1861 when the fossils of *Archaeopteryx* were discovered in a limestone quarry in Germany. At first glance scientists might have classified the find as a reptile. After all, the creature's jaw contained strong teeth, and its head and tail looked rather like those of a theropod dinosaur. But, miraculously, the fine silt that covered *Archaeopteryx* showed a complete outline of feathers. Scientists chose the name *Archaeopteryx* because it means "ancient wing."

Word Builders

- **Taxonomy** is a branch of science that gives names to species, and groups closely related species together. The word taxonomy comes from the Greek words *tassein*, which means "to put in order," and *nomia*, meaning "law."
- **Paleo-ornithologists** study ancient birds and use taxonomy in their efforts to piece together evolutionary puzzles. *Paleo* is Greek for "old."

That's Amazing!

The tallest birds ever to have walked on Earth lived in New Zealand. These were enormous birds called Moas. They stood over 10 feet (3 m) tall, higher than a basketball hoop. Humans hunted the Moas to extinction. The last known species died out before 1800.

Pathfinder

- To find out about the modern relatives of the ancient flightless birds, go to pages 20–21.
- Ancient birds such as *Hesperornis* had bills like modern birds, but they also had teeth like reptiles. The birds we see today don't have teeth—or do they? Turn to page 22 to find out.

Snow Goose

FISHING THROUGH TIME

Hesperornis was a flightless, fish-eating bird that lived over 100 million years ago, during the Cretaceous period. It was nearly 5 feet (1.5 m) tall and had teeth like *Archaeopteryx*. Its fossil was discovered in 1870 in Kansas in the U.S.A.

PLAINS STALKER

The Terror-Bird is appropriately named. It stood over 9 feet (2.7 m) tall, and it stalked the grasslands of South America. Its head was as large as that of a present-day horse.

A PIT OF GOLD

Fossils of the vulturelike *Teratornis merriami* were found at the Rancho La Brea tar pits in California, along with those of 104 other species of ancient birds.

TELL-TAIL SIGNS

Confuciusornis was found in China. This bird is believed to be 65 million years old. The fossil shows the remains of two creatures—their skeletons and the blackish outlines of their feathered bodies. One of the birds has a long pair of quills projecting from its tail. Scientists think that the long-tailed fossil may have been a male, because in most modern birds, the male has the longer tail.

CLINGING ON

A Hoatzin nestling has three claws on the end of its wings. They drop off when the bird grows older. *Archaeopteryx* and *Confuciusornis* also had three separate claws on their wing fingers. Scientists often compare features they see in fossils with creatures that are alive today in the hope of discovering more about the history of life on Earth.

Inner Workings

BIRDS NEED WINGS to fly, but wings are only one reason for their skillful soaring ability. Every part of a flying bird's body—from its heart and lungs to its light bones—is well adapted to make flight possible. But flying requires an enormous amount of energy. To make that energy, birds need lots of food, lots of oxygen, and an efficient system to get these fuel-making materials to their muscles.

A bird's respiratory or breathing system is amazingly well organized. When a bird flies, it breathes in and out with each beat of its wings. From the lungs, oxygen gets into the bloodstream. The blood, rich in oxygen and in sugars from the bird's food, is pumped by a powerful heart to the bird's muscles. The muscles then burn the oxygen and the sugars to create the energy the bird needs for flight.

A bird's lungs are connected to many air sacs that extend into its abdomen and large bones. Air in these sacs helps keep the bird's busy engine cool. The sacs also help to keep the bird's body light and evenly balanced for flight.

A bird's skeleton and feathers also play an important part in flight. A bird's body is compact and made of light bones. And the feathers provide a smooth surface so that the bird can slice gracefully through the air with the least amount of wind resistance.

THE BARE BONES

Compared to a reptile or mammal, a bird has fewer bones. Parts of its backbone are fused together, helping to provide a sturdy, compact frame for flying. A bird's collarbone is also fused into a furculum, which most people call a wishbone. As the bird flies, this bone acts like a spring, bending together to store energy when the wings come down, then releasing energy on the upstroke.

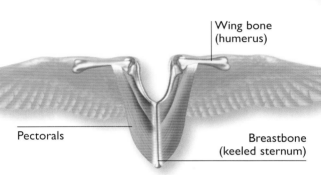

Wing bone (humerus)

Pectorals

Breastbone (keeled sternum)

POWER TO THE WINGS

Most of a bird's weight is in the center of its body, where the heavy flight muscles (pectorals) power its wings. The ends of these muscles are connected to the wing bone and to the sternum or breastbone. A bird's sternum is broad and curved like the keel of a ship, and it provides a secure anchor for the powerful muscles that give the bird strength enough to fly.

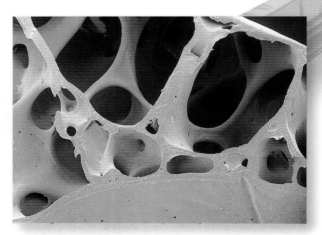

LIGHT AND STRONG

If a bird had solid bones like ours, it would be too heavy to fly. So most birds have bones that are hollow and light. You might think that hollow bones would bend or break easily, but in fact, they are amazingly strong. Inside, they have a honeycomb structure which adds lots of strength but only a little weight.

HANDS ON
Counting Beats

The rate of a bird's heartbeat is usually faster than our own. To find your heartbeat, take your index finger and middle finger and place them together, either on the side of your neck (next to your windpipe) or on your wrist, just on the other side of your wrist bones along the length of your forearm. Use a watch or a timer to see how many times your heart beats in one minute. Do this while you are sitting down.

How many times did you count? About 70? Now jump up and down, or do jumping jacks for two minutes and count again. How many times did you count? About 120? These numbers are normal for us but very low for a bird. A hummingbird's heart may beat over 700 times a minute and can sound like a cat purring.

Word Builders

- Biologists study life and living things. The word **biology** comes from two Greek words. *Bios* means "life," and *logos* means "word" or "study."
- **Vertebrae** are the connected bones that make up the spine. The Latin word *vertebra* means "a joint." This word is related to *vertare*, which means "to turn." At a joint, bones are connected in a way that allows them to turn.

That's Amazing!

- In 1758, a famous English surgeon named John Hunter found that a bird with a blocked windpipe could still breathe if it had a hole in a wing bone or leg bone. This led to the discovery of birds' complex, connected system of lungs, bones, and air sacs.
- Some ancient birds had teeth, but none of today's birds do. Teeth would make the front of a bird heavier, and therefore less capable of flight.

Pathfinder

- Everyone knows that birds have feathers, but what are feathers made of? Turn to pages 14–15.
- Birds' powerful muscles, light bones, keeled sternum, and efficient heart and lungs give them the power to fly. But how do they fly? See pages 18–19.
- To see how a bird develops from an egg into a fully grown bird, turn to pages 30–31 and 32–33.

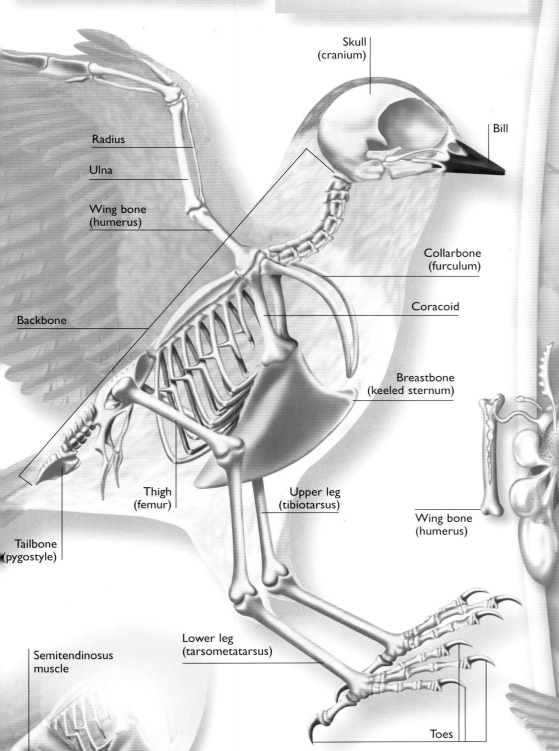

Radius
Ulna
Wing bone (humerus)
Backbone
Tailbone (pygostyle)
Semitendinosus muscle
Thigh (femur)
Lower leg (tarsometatarsus)
Flexor muscles
Flexor tendon
Skull (cranium)
Bill
Collarbone (furculum)
Coracoid
Breastbone (keeled sternum)
Upper leg (tibiotarsus)
Wing bone (humerus)
Toes

LEG MUSCLES

All birds, whether adapted for perching, running, or swimming, have two powerful muscles in the legs that control movement. These muscles are in the top part of the leg, near a bird's center of gravity. They connect to the toes by long tendons that stretch over the ankle.

INTERNAL ORGANS

THE PUMP OF LIFE

Birds' hearts are much like our own, with two pumps working to move blood through the body. On the left side, oxygen-rich blood (yellow) is pumped from the lungs into the body. On the right side, oxygen-poor blood (blue) is pumped from the body to the lungs to receive more oxygen.

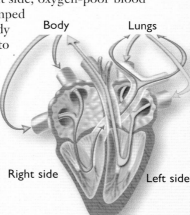

Body
Lungs
Right side
Left side

Trachea
Air sac
Wing bone (humerus)
Lung
Air sac

BREATHING DEEP

Birds have small, rigid lungs compared with humans. But the air sacs connected to the lungs help them work more efficiently. The sacs extend into birds' bones.

FUELING THE SYSTEM

Food travels down the esophagus to the crop, where it may be stored, or directly to the gizzard, which grinds food to a pulp. In the intestines, the bloodstream picks up fuel and carries it to the muscles. Wastes pass out through the cloaca.

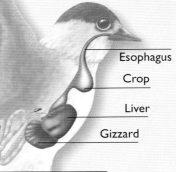

Esophagus
Crop
Liver
Gizzard
Intestines
Cloaca

Cockatiel's wing feather *Pheasant's tail feather* *Macaw's body feather* *Eagle's down feather*

Fascinating Feathers

BIRDS ARE THE only animals that have feathers. Feathers cover most of a bird's body, and they perform many important tasks. They can protect a bird from the heat and cold, and from water. They give a bird color and shape so that it can attract a mate, or hide from an enemy. And feathers are also a bird's main tool for flight.

There are three main kinds of feathers. Closest to the body are the down feathers. These light, fluffy feathers protect a bird from the cold. Over the down are the contour feathers. These are short and round. They are tougher than down, and they help give a bird its sleek, streamlined shape when flying.

The flight feathers on a bird's wings and tail are the most important for flying. The vanes of these feathers are locked together by tiny hooklets, so they are smooth and airtight when a bird is flying. When a bird wants to slow down or land, it spreads these feathers to create a drag. Swimming birds, such as penguins, use these same feathers to help them travel under the water.

Scapulars

Crest

Crown

Alula

INSIDE STORY
Feather Sleuth

Birds sometimes collide with aircraft. This can cause damage to jet engines, and may even cause a crash. So it is important for an airline to know which species of bird was involved so that any future accidents can be avoided. Who do the airlines call to investigate? Roxie Laybourne, a researcher at the Smithsonian Institution in Washington, D.C. in the United States of America.

Laybourne has been studying the structure of feathers for 40 years, and she has collected thousands of feather samples. As each kind of bird has a distinctive feather composition, she can usually uncover the identity of the culprit from just a few plumes. Laybourne has even helped solve crimes by humans where feathers have been presented as evidence.

THE ONLY WAY TO FLY
The body feathers of this Blue Jay, like those of all flying birds, point backward and neatly overlap each other. This creates a streamlined effect, allowing air to flow smoothly over the feathers when the bird is flying. If the feathers faced forward, they would catch the wind, create a drag, and make flying impossible. On the wings and tail, the bases of these important flight feathers are protected by covert feathers. The feathers that form a bridge between the back of the bird and the wing feathers are called scapulars.

BATH TIME
Feathers are important to a bird's survival, so they have to be kept in peak condition. Birds groom themselves every day, and they have developed a range of preening methods to clean and repair their feathers.

A GOOD SOAK
Bathing in water is a common preening method. This Mute Swan is cleaning its plumage by shaking itself around in the water. A good bath can also help cool a bird that is overheated.

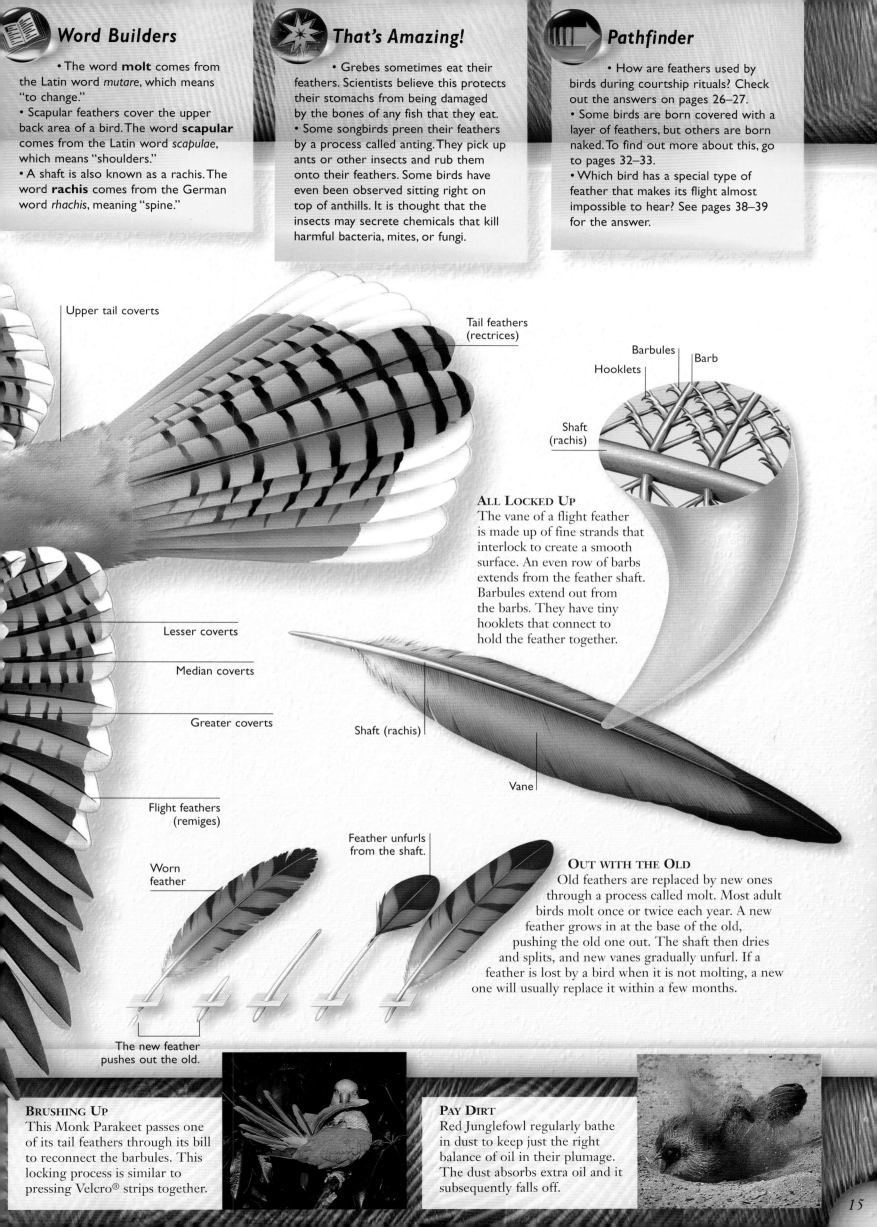

Word Builders

- The word **molt** comes from the Latin word *mutare*, which means "to change."
- Scapular feathers cover the upper back area of a bird. The word **scapular** comes from the Latin word *scapulae*, which means "shoulders."
- A shaft is also known as a rachis. The word **rachis** comes from the German word *rhachis*, meaning "spine."

That's Amazing!

- Grebes sometimes eat their feathers. Scientists believe this protects their stomachs from being damaged by the bones of any fish that they eat.
- Some songbirds preen their feathers by a process called anting. They pick up ants or other insects and rub them onto their feathers. Some birds have even been observed sitting right on top of anthills. It is thought that the insects may secrete chemicals that kill harmful bacteria, mites, or fungi.

Pathfinder

- How are feathers used by birds during courtship rituals? Check out the answers on pages 26–27.
- Some birds are born covered with a layer of feathers, but others are born naked. To find out more about this, go to pages 32–33.
- Which bird has a special type of feather that makes its flight almost impossible to hear? See pages 38–39 for the answer.

Upper tail coverts

Tail feathers (rectrices)

Barbules

Barb

Hooklets

Shaft (rachis)

ALL LOCKED UP

The vane of a flight feather is made up of fine strands that interlock to create a smooth surface. An even row of barbs extends from the feather shaft. Barbules extend out from the barbs. They have tiny hooklets that connect to hold the feather together.

Lesser coverts

Median coverts

Greater coverts

Shaft (rachis)

Flight feathers (remiges)

Vane

Feather unfurls from the shaft.

Worn feather

OUT WITH THE OLD

Old feathers are replaced by new ones through a process called molt. Most adult birds molt once or twice each year. A new feather grows in at the base of the old, pushing the old one out. The shaft then dries and splits, and new vanes gradually unfurl. If a feather is lost by a bird when it is not molting, a new one will usually replace it within a few months.

The new feather pushes out the old.

BRUSHING UP

This Monk Parakeet passes one of its tail feathers through its bill to reconnect the barbules. This locking process is similar to pressing Velcro® strips together.

PAY DIRT

Red Junglefowl regularly bathe in dust to keep just the right balance of oil in their plumage. The dust absorbs extra oil and it subsequently falls off.

Brilliant Plumage

A BEAUTIFUL BIRD flashes by and captures your attention. But how can you identify that bird? The entire feathery covering of a bird is called plumage. The plumage of each bird species is a distinctive color and shape, and provides valuable clues to help you find out the name of the bird you've just glimpsed.

The color of plumage is produced by two kinds of pigments—carotenoids and melanins—and by the structure of the feathers themselves. Carotenoids make the colors red, orange, and yellow. Melanins make black to pale brown. A combination of these two pigment types creates even more colors—except for blues and purples. These colors only occur if the feathers are structured so that they can scatter and reflect light in a special way.

Plumage comes in all shapes and colors for many reasons. It allows birds to identify other birds from their own species, and to communicate with them. It also serves as camouflage, helping birds to hide within their habitat. Male birds usually have brighter colors and use their plumage to attract a female. Some birds puff up their plumage to ward off other birds that may be encroaching on their territory.

The male Indian Peafowl, widely known as the peacock, has extraordinary plumage. He spreads more than 200 train feathers to form a 6-foot (1.8-m) fan adorned with patterns that look like eyes.

TECHNICOLOR DREAM COATS

There are 43 bird of paradise species. Each is spectacularly colored and shaped. The male Raggiana Bird of Paradise lives in Papua New Guinea. His body feathers are an orange-red color, and his head feathers are yellow, green, and black. The long feathers on his flanks, the lower part of a bird's sides, shimmer in the sunlight. When the male is not displaying his feathers, he keeps them sleek against his body.

INSIDE STORY

A Feather in the Cap

Many peoples throughout history have used birds' feathers for decoration. Today some tribes in Papua New Guinea still wear the plumes of birds of paradise during their dances and ceremonies. The tribes' hunters select and kill only a few adult male birds, leaving many younger birds to reproduce. But elsewhere in the world, other cultures have not behaved so responsibly. In the 1800s, the fashion for using feathers to

decorate ladies' hats resulted in millions of birds being shot. Some species died out altogether—they became extinct. The first Audubon Societies in America were formed in the early 1900s in protest against the killing of egrets for their fancy plumes. The work of these societies led to the formation of hundreds of groups devoted to the important job of protecting birds—especially those in danger of extinction.

PAINT A PICTURE

The black feathers on the male Wilson's Bird of Paradise make his bright colors look even more vivid. His blue cap, yellow nape, and scarlet back look as though they have been painted on him

• The word **plumage** is from the Latin word *pluma*, meaning "soft feather." **Plume** means "pen" as well as "feather," because the shafts, or quills, of some bird feathers used to be dipped in ink and used for writing.
• **Iridescent** comes from the Greek word *iris*, meaning "rainbow." Iris is also the colored portion of a human eye, and it is the name of a flower.

• The color of a bird's plumage is sometimes the result of the food it eats. The Greater Flamingo and the Roseate Spoonbill must eat the right kinds of crustaceans and microscopic food from the seabed or they will lose their bright pink coloration.
• Birds see the same range of colors that we do, but they also see ultraviolet light. Colors may appear more intense to them than they do to us.

• Plumage color and pattern give some birds extraordinary camouflage abilities. Which night bird can disguise itself as a stump of wood during the day? Go to page 38.
• Which species of bird turns white during winter to blend in with the snow? Turn to page 61 to find out.

COLORFUL ILLUSIONS

Female birds are usually less colorful than males, mainly so that they can remain hidden from predators when they are incubating eggs or rearing young. Both the colors and patterns of their plumage help birds blend in with their habitat.

SECRET TREASURES

The faces and body feathers of male and female Resplendent Quetzals look similar, but the male is more iridescent and he has long tail streamers. Like many rain forest birds, these quetzals are often hard to spot among the lush, sun-dappled foliage.

MIRROR MAGIC

The female Harlequin Duck is plain, but the male has white markings. This is called ruptive coloration and is a subtle form of camouflage. The male can be difficult to see against surfaces that are not a solid color, such as rippling water.

TURNING BLUE

Most of the year, the male Indigo Bunting is brown, like the female, and is difficult to see in his scrub habitat. But during the mating season, he sheds his drab plumage and turns a glorious blue.

HIDE IN PLAIN SIGHT

The fine patterns on the plumage of the male and female Pin-tailed Sandgrouse help conceal them among the sand, pebbles, and sparse vegetation of their dry habitat.

DANCING IN THE TREES

In a dance designed to attract a female, the male Blue Bird of Paradise makes himself look larger by raising his azure wings and long, black tail feathers. All birds of paradise have special dances that display their plumage to the best advantage.

Indian flying fox (bat)

Blue morpho butterfly (insect)

Flying dragon (lizard)

Flying gurnard (fish)

Rulers of the Sky

BIRDS ARE THE most amazing flying creatures on Earth. Insects and bats can fly, too, and some lizards, frogs, and squirrels can glide. But few can fly as high or as far or as fast as a bird. Birds may use flight to find food, to get away from enemies, or to migrate thousands of miles.

Most birds flap their wings to stay airborne, using their tail to help them change direction. But some birds are better at hovering, swooping, or gliding than others. The shape and size of a bird's wings determine the kind of flight to which it is best suited.

Birds with small, short, rounded wings are best suited for short flights, although they sometimes migrate hundreds of miles. Birds with longer wings can take advantage of air currents to travel far. Albatrosses have very long, narrow wings. They can use the wild energy generated by the interaction between wind and waves to stay airborne. They rise on powerful updrafts, and when they can go no higher, they glide down. To get lift again, they simply dip one wing and bank sharply into another updraft. This kind of flying is called dynamic soaring. The great arcs of this flight pattern look like a series of rainbows laid end to end.

GOING UP

Bird wings are nearly flat underneath and curved across the top. This means that air must travel more quickly across the top than across the bottom as the bird flies forward. This creates a lower pressure above the wing, providing the lift that keeps the bird in the air.

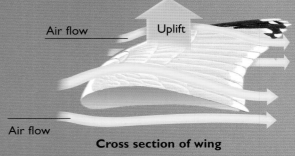

Air flow   Uplift

Air flow

Cross section of wing

HIGHER AND HIGHER

The Wandering Albatross has the largest wingspan of any bird—up to 11 feet (3.3 m) wide. This seabird can fly effortlessly over the southern oceans, where strong winds and gales are common. While traveling for hundreds of miles in search of food, it can glide for hours without beating its wings.

INSIDE STORY
Dreaming of Flight

Since ancient times, humans have wanted to fly. They admired birds and sometimes worshipped them. The brilliant Italian inventor and artist named Leonardo da Vinci (1452–1519) was ahead of his time in thinking about how humans could fly. He closely observed birds in flight, and studied how their bodies were constructed. Then he sketched designs for wings that look surprisingly similar to today's aircraft. But in Leonardo's time there were no engines that could power flight. It took another 400 years before two brothers, Orville and Wilbur Wright, successfully flew the world's first airplane, the *Flyer*, in 1903.

American Crow

TO FLAP OR NOT TO FLAP?

Wings folded

Scarlet Minivet

BEST WINGS FORWARD
Birds flap their wings to stay in the air and move forward. Huge muscles power the stroke, pulling the wings forward and down and upward and back. The downstroke takes more energy and gives lift. The upstroke isn't such hard work. Feathers streamline the body, making flight easier.

A TUCK IN TIME
A small bird can fold its wings in short bursts to save energy. When flapping, the bird rises. When its wings are tucked close to its body, the bird falls. These rests are brief and hard to spot, but the bird's flight pattern is easy to see. It is up and down rather than straight forward.

Word Builders

- The word **aviation** comes from the Greek word *avis*, meaning "bird." Other words use *avi-* as their stem word: **aviator**, a pilot; **aviary**, a large bird cage; and **aviculture**, the rearing or keeping of birds.
- The name **albatross** is a variation of the Portuguese word *alcatraz*, meaning "seafowl." The *c* may have been changed to a *b* because of the bird's coloring—the Latin word for white is *alba*.

That's Amazing!

It is difficult to measure how fast a bird can fly because it depends upon the circumstances under which the bird is traveling. Some birds can fly as fast as small airplanes when they are being chased, or are chasing. In 1961, a pilot clocked a male Red-breasted Merganser, startled by his plane, flying up to 80 miles per hour (129 km/h). Peregrine Falcons can reach speeds above 110 miles per hour (180 km/h) when diving for prey.

Pathfinder

- To learn more about the muscles that allow birds to take off, fly, and land, turn to pages 12–13.
- Which bird has a special wing design that makes it hard for its prey to hear its approaching flight? See pages 38–39.
- How far do birds fly when migrating? The answers are on pages 40–41.

HITTING THE BRAKES

Birds need to fly fast in order to stay in the air. To land, they usually drop their tails and open out their wings. The air strikes the underside of their wings, slowing them down so they can alight safely. Airplanes open flaps on their wings during landing to accomplish the same thing.

WE HAVE LIFTOFF

Most birds seem to take off effortlessly. They simply leap into the air. But the pelican spends a lot of time in water, and that makes it more difficult for this large bird to get airborne. Using its feet to help lift its body above the water's surface, the pelican has to flap its massive wings fast to get liftoff. Once in the air, it is a strong flier and glider.

Hot air rising

Golden Eagle

HITCHING A RIDE

The most energy-efficient method of flying is to glide on rising hot air currents known as thermals. Birds with long, wide wings, such as eagles, can fly in a circular pattern to stay inside the column of rising air as they are lifted higher and higher. From a great height, they can then glide slowly downward for long distances before hitching a ride on another thermal.

HOVERING STATIONS

Some birds can hover like insects. To do this, the bird must beat its wings rapidly, then rotate them in a number of different ways at the shoulder joint. Hovering requires lots of energy. Hummingbirds such as the Purple-backed Thornbill are able to hover. They can also fly forward, backward, and straight up or down.

Purple-backed Thornbill

Grounded

IT SEEMS ONLY natural for birds to fly. But quite a few birds never take to the air. No one is sure why they developed this way. The most likely theory, though, is that they lost the ability to fly simply because they stopped needing it.

Many flightless birds evolved on remote islands, such as the Galápagos Islands or New Zealand. Island birds were safe on the ground as there were no humans or other predators such as cats, rats, or foxes. And they didn't need to fly to gather food as supplies were always close by. So they gradually quit flying because it takes so much energy. When humans and other predators arrived, flightless birds couldn't escape them. Some, like New Zealand's Moa, became extinct as the newcomers took their places in their old habitats.

Some birds lost the ability to fly and then grew huge. This happened to the Ostriches, which can grow to be about 9 feet (2.75 m) tall. They survived because they developed long, powerful legs on which they could run faster than a racehorse to escape predators. When cornered, they could also defend themselves by kicking. They still have small wings, though, which they use mainly for balance.

INSIDE STORY

Seeding the Fruit

Cassowaries are large, flightless birds that move quickly along rain forest floors. They eat large amounts of fruit, and can, after digesting, disperse seeds a long way from the parent tree. Dr. David Westcott, who works for the Tropical Forest Research Center in north Queensland, Australia, studies these birds to measure the effect they have on rain forest tree populations. To monitor a bird, Dr. Westcott catches it. He feeds it and notes how long it takes food to travel through its digestive system. Then he attaches a radio transmitter and releases the bird into the wild. Dr. Westcott tracks the birds and notes where they drop seeds in their waste. He learns more about how cassowaries live, and can measure the way they affect the rain forest's ecology.

FLYING UNDERWATER

There are 18 species of penguins, and none of them can fly. The largest is the Emperor Penguin, which lives in Antarctica. It endures temperatures as low as -80°F (-62°C) during the bleakest winter months. All penguins have small, stiff, flipperlike wings. These wings enable them to be superb swimmers. Penguins dive into the water to catch their food, surfacing often to breathe. They can travel underwater at speeds of up to 20 miles per hour (32 km/h).

FLIGHTLESS IN NEW ZEALAND

There are five flightless birds living in New Zealand's Fiordland National Park—the Little Penguin, Kakapo, Takahe, Weka, and Brown Kiwi. The Kiwi is the country's national bird. It is nocturnal, and is one of only a few bird species to have a good sense of smell.

The Kakapo is the largest parrot in the world, and the only one that cannot fly. It can, however, climb trees and glide to the ground. Because it lives on the ground and nests in holes, it is vulnerable to predators—there are fewer than 50 still alive.

Word Builders

Kakapo, **Weka**, and **Kiwi** are names taken from the Maori language. The Maoris were the first humans to live on the islands of New Zealand. *Kakapo* is a combination of two Maori words, *kaka*, meaning "parrot," and *po,* meaning "night." *Weka* means "hen." *Kiwi* was originally the name the Maoris gave the country. The name was then given to the bird that became New Zealand's national mascot. *Kiwi* is also a nickname given to all New Zealanders.

That's Amazing!

• The Emperor Penguin can dive to a depth of up to 1,750 feet (530 m), and can stay underwater for nearly 20 minutes.
• The female Brown Kiwi lays enormous eggs, which are almost one-sixth of her own body weight. These eggs take 11 weeks to incubate, the longest time for any bird. In comparison, Yellow-breasted Chats' eggs take just 11 days, and chickens' eggs take 21 days.

Pathfinder

• The Ostrich lays the largest egg. Which bird lays the smallest? See page 31.
• The Brown Kiwi is a nocturnal bird. What does this mean? Are there other nocturnal birds? See page 38–39.
• Many birds, not just flightless ones, are in danger of extinction. To find out more about birds in danger, turn to pages 44–45.
• Which bird is known as the "penguin of the north?" Turn to page 49.

Emu

Ostrich

Rhea

INTERNATIONAL RELATIONS

Rheas, the Emu, and the Ostrich are very large flightless birds. They live on the continents of South America, Australia, and Africa, respectively. Because they look alike, it's possible they came from a common ancestor when the continents were joined. Or they may have evolved to be so similar to one another because they all live in open grassland, and feed on grass and insects.

The Takahe is a large, flightless rail. It was thought to have been extinct for 50 years, but in 1948, a small number were found. Today, there are about 180 Takahes living in a grassy hillside reserve near Te Anau. These solitary birds nest between tufts of grass, but live in the forests during winter.

The Weka is a flightless rail that has well-developed wings, but only uses them for balance when running. It survives because it is a strong fighter. Wekas are known to kill rats as well as other birds that live on the ground.

Bills and Feet

TRY TO PICK up an apple without using your hands. It's not easy. Birds don't have hands. They use their bills and feet to hold what they eat, to move things around, to scratch for food, and to defend themselves. The size and shape of a bird's bill and feet can tell you a lot about the bird's lifestyle.

    The upper half of a bird's bill is called the maxilla, and the lower half is called the mandible—although the term mandible is often used for both. The bill is made of keratin, the same substance of which feathers are made. The Pileated Woodpecker's strong, straight bill is ideal for hammering into tree bark to dislodge insects. The Palm Cockatoo uses its stout bill to crush fruit, seeds, and berries, and the Far Eastern Curlew finds food by probing deep into the mud flats of waterways with its long, curved bill. The African Spoonbill has a flat, round bulge on the end of its long bill. It sweeps the floor of a lake with its lower mandible, and then traps food between the two spoonlike tips. The Bald Eagle has a hook-shaped bill, well designed to tear apart prey.

    The upper part of a bird's leg is covered by body feathers. The lower part is covered by small scales. The joint that seems to be halfway up its leg is its ankle. Extending from the ankle is a long foot, then two, three or four toes. Birds use these toes in many different ways.

HOLDING ON
Birds do not have real teeth. The Common Merganser, however, has a row of spikes on both mandibles that point backward. The bird uses these serrated edges and the hooked tip of its bill to hold on to slippery fishes.

SPEAR FISHING
The bill, head, and neck are all that can be seen of the Anhinga when it swims with its body submerged. This is why it is sometimes known as the "snakebird." It dives underwater to spear fishes on its sharp bill before resurfacing to feed.

HANDS ON
Collecting Footprints

When birds walk on wet ground, they leave behind telltale tracks. To make a cast of a bird's footprints, mix about 1½ cups of plaster of paris with 1 cup of water in a bucket. When the mixture is smooth, pour it over the footprints. When the cast has hardened sufficiently, lift it up and leave it in a safe place to dry completely. Then brush off any sand or dirt. Now try to identify the species of bird that left the prints.

Word Builders

• More than half the world's birds are classified as passerines. They are able to perch. The word **passerine** comes from the Latin *passerinus*, meaning "sparrowlike."
• The word **mandible** comes from the Latin *mandere*, meaning "to chew." The word **maxilla** comes from a Latin word meaning "jaw."

That's Amazing!

• The Eurasian Wallcreeper is as agile as Spiderman and can climb vertically up a rock face. It has three toes pointing forward and one pointing backward, each with sharp claws that enable the bird to keep its grip.
• Egyptian Vultures use their bills to pick up stones weighing up to 2 pounds (1 kg). They drop them onto Ostrich eggs, cracking open the thick shells so they can eat the contents.

Pathfinder

• Which bird turns its head upside down to strain its food from water in its specially adapted bill? Turn to pages 8–9 to find out more.
• Birds do not have teeth, so how do they grind their food? See page 13.
• One bird is so skilled in using its bill that it can weave leaves together to make its nest. Go to pages 28–29.

BEST FOOT FORWARD

The reptilian ancestors of birds had five toes, and their feet were well adapted to walking on the ground. Today, birds' feet have evolved into a variety of shapes for different tasks such as swimming, climbing, perching, and running, as well as landing and taking off.

PADDLE PERFECT

The Mallard has webbed feet, like all other ducks. The skin between their toes lets them use their feet like paddles when they are in water.

EXACT CONTROL

The Toco Toucan's large bill has made this bird famous worldwide. Despite its size, the hollow bill is remarkably light. It is strengthened internally by a honeycomblike support similar to that found in the bones of flying birds. The toucan picks up food in the tip of its bill. It moves the food into position with its tongue, which is about 6 inches (15 cm) long with brushlike bristles on the end. Once the food is in the right position, the toucan throws its head back and tosses the food down its throat. Toucans have two toes pointing forward and two pointing backward, giving the bird a good grip on branches while it feeds.

PADDED FOR COMFORT

Rheas are very large, heavy birds with powerful legs. Because they do not fly, their feet do a lot of hard work. Extra flesh on the feet helps absorb the impact of the bird's weight when it is running.

TWIST AND TURN

The African Gymnogene is a bird of prey with unique legs. It can bend its legs at extraordinary angles. Because it can twist 70 degrees behind and 30 degrees from side to side, it can forage in enclosed places such as tree hollows, which its prey might mistakenly think are safe havens.

GETTING A GRIP

The Black-capped Lorikeet has two toes pointing forward and two turned backward. This allows the bird to grasp a branch firmly, and to hold food securely when it is feeding.

WALKING ON WATER

Northern Jacanas are wading birds. They have long toes and claws, so they can walk on lily leaves and other floating plants without sinking.

23

The Way Birds Act

A BIRD SWOOPS past you, heading off to perform some important task. Is it trying to find material for building a nest? Does it have young to feed? Is it about to migrate to a warmer climate? Every action a bird makes tells us something fascinating about the way it lives its life. Look more closely and you'll see that behavior that seems strange to us makes perfect sense to a bird.

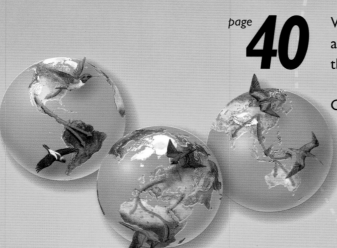

All Dressed Up

MALE BIRDS WORK hard to attract a mate. One of the most common and obvious ways they do this is to display their bright plumage to its best advantage. Yes, they're showing off. It's called courting. They want to persuade a female to ignore all the other males and pay attention only to them. Birds court for the same reason that people date. Most are looking for partners to help them raise their families.

Some male birds rely on more than their good looks to find a mate. They may select a territory, or home area, and build a nest there. The male bowerbird even builds a stage on which it can perform for the females it is trying to attract. The Golden Bowerbird creates its stage on a platform that is more than 3 feet (1 m) off the ground.

Each species of bird has its own rituals. Many male birds make distinctive sounds and sing songs. Some bring gifts. Male herons, anhingas, and birds of prey often present the females with sticks for their nests. Magnificent aerial displays or dancelike routines with their intended partner are also part of some birds' display strategy. Albatrosses nibble on each others' necks, a practice known as allopreening.

After mating, many birds stay together to incubate the eggs and raise their young. But in some species, the females raise their young by themselves.

STARS OF THE STAGE

Male bowerbirds are talented designers and interior decorators. They build a stage area where they can perform dances and present gifts to potential mates. Vogelkop Gardener Bowerbirds are skilled architects and create the most elaborate bower of all—a large, hutlike structure. All male bowerbirds decorate their stage areas with bright objects, such as shells, fruits, flower petals, or even bottlecaps and broken glass. They busy themselves arranging and rearranging the objects to make the bower as attractive as possible. Once the male has attracted and mated with a female, she builds a separate nest for the eggs, with no help from the male.

RED ALERT
After a male Great Frigatebird has constructed a nest, he inflates his red throat pouch, shakes his wings, and calls to circling females by making loud, gobbling noises.

DANCING DAYS

THE LONGEST WALTZ
Each year albatrosses renew their bonds with the partner they have chosen for life by performing complex mating rituals. These can last for days and usually involve both birds. The male Royal Albatross has a special, elaborate display. He begins by stretching out his massive wings and throwing his head and bill up toward the sky. Next, he lowers his head and marches around the nest like a toy soldier. Then he cocks his tail and shivers like a dog shaking off water.

Word Builders

• When birds **preen**, they clean and oil their feathers. The word is related to *prune*, "to trim away." In the word **allopreening**, *allo-* is a prefix from the Greek word "other." When birds allopreen, they clean each other's feathers.
• **Territory** comes from the Latin word *territorium*, which means "the land around a town." *Territorium*, in turn, comes from the Latin word *terra*, meaning "land."

That's Amazing!

• In a few bird species, the female has plumage more colorful than the male's. Among phalaropes, the females are the more brightly colored and use their plumage to attract a mate. The males care for the young, and their dull colors help hide them from predators.
• Albatrosses take one partner for life. But after most hummingbirds mate, they may not see their partners again.

Pathfinder

• The male bird that displays the finest feathers usually gets a mate. But how do birds keep their feathers in peak condition? See pages 14–15.
• Which male bird has feathers that shimmer in the sunlight when he is displaying? Turn to pages 16–17.
• Some male birds sing during courtship. To learn more about songbirds, turn to page 53.

INSIDE STORY
Shooting Stars

Film allows bird watchers to study and understand birds in distant parts of the world. But a lot of patience is required when trying to capture birds in their natural surroundings. For instance, during courtship, several male manakins gather in a lek—a place where they display for females. If you manage to find a lek to film, you also have to be there at the right time to see the males displaying. When photographer Marie Read set out to record Long-tail Manakins in their leks, she visited the dense forests of Costa Rica several times before she was successful. Read then shot a series of beautiful and informative photographs of the manakins' elaborate leapfrogging dance. Since then, she has also documented the Red-capped and Golden-collared Manakins in their leks.

FAN MALE
In the breeding season, male Great Egrets grow long, white feathers, called aigrettes, on their backs. The birds spread them like a fan to entice the female.

SYNCHRONIZED BALLET

Western Grebes perform a beautiful series of dances together on top of the water. Early in the nesting season, the two birds stage a little ballet, holding long strands of vegetation in their bills. This is called weed dancing. At the height of courtship, they rise in a graceful pose, called rushing, and run across the water's surface for some distance before diving below. Rival males also use this dance to defend their territories.

IN A WHIRL

Many raptors, such as these African Fish-Eagles, perform incredible aerial feats during courtship. The bonding pair may fly together in circles, or in tandem, one above the other. They may even hook talons and do cartwheels in midair like circus acrobats. Two rival males may also lock talons when they are battling over the right to a territory.

A Nesting Instinct

HAVE YOU EVER looked closely at a nest and wondered how the bird knew how to build such a useful, clever container? Scientists believe that nest-building skills are an example of instinctive behavior because they are not learned from other birds. Each kind of bird just knows how to make its nest.

The nests we see today are the result of millions of years of evolution. In the distant past, some birds' ancestors simply covered eggs in soil or rotting vegetation to keep them warm, while others used natural cavities in trees as a place to lay their eggs. As birds began to use their body heat to incubate their eggs, they gradually developed the skills needed for more sophisticated nest building.

Most birds construct a nest of some sort. If you have seen one, it was probably cup-shaped and made of twigs or grass. But there are hundreds of kinds of nests, all with different designs and built with a variety of materials. Some are just scrapes in the sand or big piles of sticks. Some are tiny, weighing not much more than a paper cup. Others are enormous and can be the weight of a horse. Many contain found objects, such as hair, paper, foil, string, or feathers.

Cliff Swallows make jugs out of mud, attaching them to bridges. Puffins and kingfishers dig tunnels and place their nests inside. Orioles build deep baskets that hang from tree forks. Bushtits create long sacks from twigs, roots, and moss that they paste together with spiderwebs. No matter what their shape, nests help the adult birds keep their eggs warm, and most protect the eggs and chicks from predators.

HANDS ON
Making a Nest

Birds are master weavers. To appreciate their amazing skills, try building your own nest.

❶ You will need a stick that has a fork of two or three strong branches; lots of tiny flexible twigs; and some grass, leaves, reeds, and whatever else birds may use—mud, string, dry moss, or even some of your own hair (if you have just had it cut).

❷ Arrange the twigs, using the forked branches of your stick as a foundation. You could start with a flat platform, as some birds do, or try to bend the twigs around the branches to form a cup. The idea is to make a little basket.

❸ Keep weaving material into the nest to make the sides strong. Line the nest with moss or grass.

You may make lots of nests that fall apart before you manage to come up with a good, strong design.

MASTER WEAVER

The male Black-headed Weaver, or Village Weaver, stitches strips of vegetation together to make a roofed basket. He ties knots, using grasses, to make the nest secure. Then he displays in front of the nest to attract a mate. The males usually pair with many females during the mating season. This system is called polygyny. These weavers nest in colonies. The females raise their young alone and work with other females in the colony to look out for predators. The seeds that the Black-headed Weaver eats are in very rich supply, so the males have no need to defend a territory and food source.

Word Builders

• Cavity nesters are birds that nest in holes in trees or cliffs, or in bird boxes. These holes are called cavities. **Cavity** comes from the Latin word *cavus*, meaning "a hollow place."
• Some birds practice polygyny, in which one male mates with many females. The word **polygyny** comes from the Greek words *poly*, meaning "many," and *gyne*, meaning "female."

That's Amazing!

• Some tropical birds, such as flycatchers and wrens, nest near bees' and wasps' nests. These insects probably keep away flies and predators.
• Some birds of prey allow other birds, such as sparrows, to place nests inside their own nests, which are much larger than those of their guests. The little birds may warn the larger birds by chirping loudly when danger is near.

Pathfinder

• Which bird builds a nestlike structure that never houses eggs or young birds? Go to pages 26–27.
• How do cliff-nesting birds that don't build nests keep their eggs from rolling off into the ocean? Go to page 30.
• Which bird nests on the ledges of some of the tallest buildings in the world? See pages 46–47.

HOME SWEET HOME

PRIME REAL ESTATE
Some raptors, such as the Verreaux's Eagle of southern Africa, build large nests on cliff edges. These sites, called eyries, are sometimes used for centuries. Each year, the eagles add more twigs and other building material.

SAFE AND SOUND
The Scarlet Tanager of North America likes to build its nests in oak trees, anywhere from 8 to 75 feet (2.6 to 22.5 m) above the ground. The nests are cup-shaped, like those of most tree-nesting birds. This shape is perfect for preventing the eggs from rolling out.

WATERSIDE
Kingfishers, shelducks, and Bank Swallows burrow into riverbanks to create their nests. They dig tunnels above the waterline to avoid the risk of flooding. Other birds, such as Manx Shearwaters, use old rabbit burrows.

IN THE OVEN
The Rufous Hornero, an ovenbird, lives in South America. It builds its nest in a tree or on top of a telephone pole. The nest resembles an old-fashioned baker's oven. It is made of mud mixed with grass and animal hairs. Inside the entrance is a grass-lined chamber where the eggs are laid.

SECURE HOLDINGS
The Reed Warbler's nest is built in tall reeds, right over water, so that the young birds are safe from predators. The Reed Warbler is an excellent weaver and can make its nest incredibly secure so the young don't fall into the water on windy days.

AIMING HIGH
The Black-winged Stilt scrapes a hollow on an open, dry site or in low vegetation. Sometimes it makes a cup nest on a mud bank or mound. This nest can be built up higher if the water level rises.

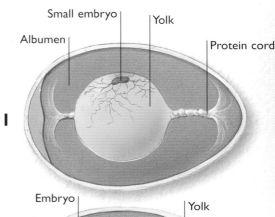

Before They Hatch

THE EGGS THAT a female bird lays may seem like lifeless things. But their smooth exterior hides something wonderful. A tiny embryo is alive inside each egg and is growing into a bird. The embryo has everything it needs to grow until it fills the egg completely and is ready to hatch. Well, almost everything. An egg will grow into a live chick only if it is incubated, which means it must be kept warm.

The female usually lays her fertilized eggs in a nest. Then, either the male or the female parent bird can keep the eggs warm, or they may share the task. Before a bird begins incubating, it may lose feathers on its belly. This area is called a brood patch. When the bird presses its brood patch against the eggs, the warmth from its body helps to keep the eggs at just the right temperature. The bird simply turns the eggs to warm them all over. A few bird species cover eggs under mounds of leaf litter and leave them to incubate.

Incubation can take just over a week for the egg of a small bird and 12 weeks for that of a large one. A chick may start to make noises several days before it hatches. To hatch, it has to peck at the shell and make a crack around the larger end. Some parent birds may hear the chick's cheeps and help to remove parts of the shell.

A PEEK INSIDE

1. An egg contains the growing bird (embryo), a yellow yolk, and albumen (egg white). The chick uses the yolk and albumen as food before it hatches.
2. As the chick uses the yolk and albumen, it produces wastes, which are stored in a special sac.
3. When the chick is close to hatching, it almost fills the entire shell.
4. Unhatched chicks have a special egg tooth that helps them break free. After they hatch, the tooth falls off.

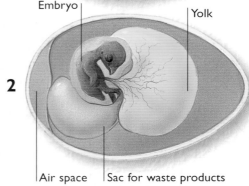

1 Small embryo   Yolk   Albumen   Protein cord

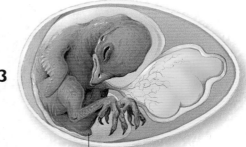

2 Embryo   Yolk   Air space   Sac for waste products

3 Developing chick

Egg tooth   **4**

HANDS ON

Egg Hideout

Children in some countries paint eggs with bright colors to use for Easter egg hunts. In the wild, most eggs are not bright at all. They need to fade into the background so they cannot be seen easily by predators.

See if you can paint eggs a color that will make them blend in with a natural environment. You will need eggs from a supermarket, a paintbrush, and watercolor paints. Look for a good nest site, perhaps some dried leaves at the base of a tree. Study the colors and patterns of the site. Then paint your eggs to match. Start with a neutral base color, such as brown or gray, then dot, streak, and blotch with greens, darker browns, or black. Now place your eggs at the site and see if a friend can find them.

DIVERSITY RULES

Birds' eggs come in many different shapes, colors, and sizes. These variations are important to the survival of each species. The variations help keep eggs safe from predators and protect them in specific environments.

GOING NOWHERE

One end of the egg of the Common Murre is narrow and pointed. This shape stops it from being accidentally knocked off the cliff edge on which it is laid. If the egg should start to roll, it will move in a circle, rather than a straight line.

Word Builders

• **Incubate** comes from the Latin word *cubare*, meaning "to lie" or "recline." *In-* is a prefix meaning "on."
• **Brood** comes from the German word *Brut*, which means "breed." A brood is a group of birds that hatch together. The verb "to brood" means to keep young birds warm by covering them up after they have hatched.

That's Amazing!

• The largest bird eggs ever found belonged to the extinct elephant birds. Their eggs could hold over two gallons (8 l) of fluid. That's the contents of two of the biggest cartons of milk you can buy from a grocery store.
• The Ostrich lays the largest egg of any living bird. Just how big is it? Try to imagine an egg that can hold the contents of 12–18 chicken eggs.

Pathfinder

• Some birds build elaborate nests to protect their unhatched eggs. Find out more on pages 28–29.
• Which bird builds mounds of leaves in which to bury its eggs to keep them warm? The answer is on page 45.
• Which male bird incubates its single egg on its feet? See page 60.

BRAVING THE NEW WORLD

It can take several days for a young chick, such as this Downy Woodpecker, to break through the tough shell of an egg. First, the chick must turn to face the blunter end of the egg. It then pierces the air space in which it lies, enabling it to breathe for the first time. Next, the chick pecks at the shell, using its egg tooth and powerful neck muscles to help it break through. The chick turns in a circle by pushing itself with its feet so that the crack it is making will run right around the shell. Once the circle is complete, the chick pushes its way out of the egg. It usually emerges headfirst.

FOSTER CARE
Some cuckoos are nest parasites, laying their eggs in other birds' nests. The nest owners may not notice, even when the cuckoo eggs are larger than their own. They will usually raise the young cuckoo.

LOOK-ALIKES
Common Terns lay their eggs right on the ground. The eggs are often hard to see among pebbles, because the spotting on the eggs blends in with the patterns on the pebbles. This is perfect camouflage.

Eurasian Bullfinch hatching

Six days old

28 days old

Fully grown at nine months old

Growing Up

THE HATCHING OF a young bird is a remarkable event. Some birds, such as ducks, are born with their eyes open. These young birds run and swim as soon as they are born. They are described as precocial. Precocial birds are already covered with downy feathers when they hatch. These are eventually replaced by their adult feathers.

Other birds, like the songbirds, are born with their eyes closed. These newborn birds are too weak to move around after they hatch. They are known as altricial birds. Most altricial birds, including the Eurasian Bullfinch, hatch naked or have a very sparse down cover. The feathers of altricial birds grow out of tracts along the bird's wings and body.

Chicks depend on older birds for food and safety until they can fend for themselves. In most species, both parents tend and feed their young. Among ducks and some other species, only the females raise the chicks. Among phalaropes, only males raise the chicks. Among Florida Scrub-Jays, the parents get help from the chicks' older brothers and sisters. Pelicans nest in large colonies. When chicks have left the nest, parents gather them in a group called a crèche. Then all the adult birds can be on the lookout for predators that might harm the young. However, pelican parents still bring food to their own chicks.

Day by day, young birds grow bigger and stronger and learn the many skills they will need to survive.

A COOL SHOWER

Although the Shoebill looks clumsy, it is surprisingly skilled and delicate in its movements. Young Shoebills are often exposed to the fierce African heat. The parent bird fetches cool, refreshing water in its enormous, hook-tipped bill and showers it over its young. At other times, it shades the young with its huge body and large, broad wings.

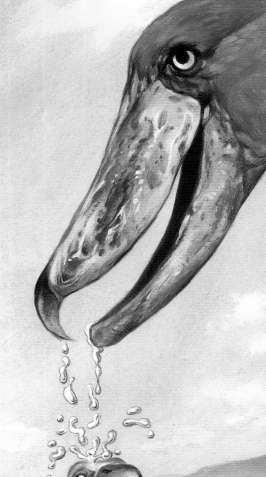

BACKING THE FUTURE
The parent bird has to work hard to keep its chicks from harm. Although the young Common Loon can swim almost from the moment it is born, it cannot fend for itself. When the parent senses danger, it carries the young bird to safety on its back.

FOOD DELIVERY SERVICE
Some young birds cannot digest solid food. Adult pelicans change food into a liquid. They let the liquid food trickle down their large bills for the young to eat. As the young grow, they begin to eat solid food from a parent's pouch.

ACTING ON CUE
The Killdeer has developed a way to trick creatures that prey on its young. It diverts the predator's attention by pretending to have a broken wing, which would make it easier to catch. Once the predator has been lured away from the nest, the Killdeer stops its pretense and flies off.

Word Builders

- **Altricial** comes from the Latin word *altricies*, which means "feeders" or "nurses." A chick that is altricial is helpless and needs a parent to care for its every need.
- **Precocial** comes from the Latin word *praecoci*, which means "ripened early." A chick that is precocial can move around and leave the nest soon after it hatches.

That's Amazing!

- In Greenland, Barnacle Geese lay their eggs on cliffs to protect them from foxes. When goslings first leave the nest, they half jump and half fly hundreds of feet to the sea below. They often hit rocks on the way down, but their body fat and soft plumage cushion the blows.
- Young male songbirds in the wild copy the male adults' songs. Caged birds seldom have the same calls as their own kind in the wild because they have not heard them sing.

Pathfinder

- A young South American rain forest nestling provides a clue about the evolution of birds. See page 11.
- The instinct to fly is strong, but how do birds manage to do what so few other vertebrates can? Find out more on pages 18–19.
- When winter approaches, many birds migrate. How do young birds learn the migration routes? Turn to pages 40–41.

SCHOOL IN SESSION

Young birds need many skills to survive. Some skills are instinctive, some are learned, and some require both instinct and learning.

DUCKS TO WATER

Water birds take to the water soon after they hatch because there are often predators waiting to catch them. Swimming is an instinctual behavior, like nest building. But a duckling needs to learn from its parent where to go to find food and shelter, and how to stay safe from predators.

COME FLY WITH ME

When fledgling Banded Honeyeaters leave the nest, they do not return. Their ability to fly is inherited, but mastering the skill takes practice. These nomadic birds need to fly well—they cover vast distances to find the flowers and blossoms on which they feed.

LET ME SHOW YOU

Young birds often pick up skills by watching and copying their parents.

Green Herons in Florida, for example, learned by accident that dropping bread into a pond attracted fish. Their young copied this skill so they could catch fish.

INSIDE STORY

Are You My Mother?

When a chick hatches, does it know what species of bird it is? Does a gosling know that it's a goose? Konrad Lorenz (1903–1989), an Austrian zoologist, explored this kind of question in his work. He set up an experiment in which he incubated some goose eggs in a laboratory incubator. When the chicks hatched, he was there to feed them, keep them warm and protect them. He even made sounds and movements like an adult goose. The goslings soon accepted him as their parent and followed him everywhere. By fooling the goslings, Lorenz showed that young birds learn who they are by a process called imprinting. That is, they attach themselves to a figure who cares for them—usually their parent—and think that they are the same kind of creature. For this ingenious experiment and many others in animal behavior, Lorenz won a Nobel Prize in 1973.

Eating Like a Bird

IF SOMEONE SAYS, "you eat like a bird," they mean you pick at your food and eat very little. But in fact, birds eat a lot more food than humans do when you compare their body size with the amount of food they consume. Birds have to eat lots to supply the energy they need for flying, building nests, and keeping warm in winter.

Birds eat all kinds of things—seeds, fruits, and plants, as well as animals called invertebrates. These include worms, clams, shrimps, and insects. The size and shape of birds' bills and feet vary according to what they usually eat. The Tufted Titmouse has strong feet for gripping thin twigs while hanging at difficult angles to reach insects on leaves. Warblers have slender bills for delving among leafy branches to find juicy caterpillars. Birds such as flycatchers, swifts, swallows, and nightjars, which eat mostly insects, have a wide, rather gaping bill. When flying, these birds open their bills and use them to catch the insects.

For some birds, it can be a challenge to find the food they eat. Limpkins and Snail Kites are particular about their diet, living mainly on snails. For the seed and fruit eaters, it can be difficult to find enough food in winter or when plants fail to bear fruit. Waxwings and crossbills are nomadic in their hunt for food. They travel beyond their nesting areas after they have finished all the pine cones or berries there.

HANDS ON
Feed the Birds

To make a simple bird feeder, you will need a clean, dry plastic milk carton, one straight stick or dowel, scissors, and some string.

❶ On one side of the carton, about 1 inch (2.5 cm) from the bottom, cut out a 3-inch (7.5-cm) square opening. Make a second square on the opposite side of the carton.

❷ Just below each opening, punch a hole into which your stick or dowel will fit. Push the stick or dowel through the holes to make a perch for the birds.

❸ Fill the bottom of the feeder, up to the level of the openings, with seed, fresh fruit, or meal worms. Tie one end of the string onto the handle of the carton, and hang the feeder from a tree or post.

FRUITS AND NUTS TO GO
The Rhinoceros Hornbill of Malaya and Thailand often wanders through the forest in search of its favorite fruits and nuts. Hornbills can easily handle large fruit and open the tough husks of nuts with their enormous bills.

IT'S ALL IN THE METHOD

CATCH OF THE DAY
Sometimes the tastiest tidbits require a little extra effort. Oystercatchers feed mostly on the shellfishes that they find on mud flats and beaches. The Eurasian Oystercatcher opens the shells of mussels and oysters with its stout, chisel-like bill. It either stabs and cuts the muscle that holds the two halves of the shell together, or it shatters the shell against a rock.

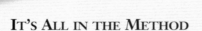

HITTING THE MARK
The Red-breasted Sapsucker drills row upon row of small holes into trees that produce sap. Each hole is drilled at an incline so that the sap can drip out. The bird eats the sap, along with any insects that are attracted to it, mopping them up with its bristle-covered tongue.

Word Builders

• The Latin suffix -*vore* means "eating." Birds that eat insects are known as **insectivores**, while birds that eat fruit, which is *frux* in Latin, are called **frugivores**.

• **Invertebrates** are animals that do not have backbones. The word is derived from the Latin prefix *in-*, which means "without," and the Latin word *vertebratus*, meaning "jointed."

That's Amazing!

Some birds and plants have evolved so closely that their habits help each other to survive. For example, Clark's Nutcrackers rely on the fruit of the whitebark pine as a winter food. They bury the fruit by the thousands in late summer, then dig it up to eat in the winter. Buried fruit that is not eaten in the winter may sprout in the spring, helping the pine to reproduce. These new trees will provide food for future generations of Clark's Nutcrackers.

Pathfinder

• Birds do not have teeth to grind food, so how is food processed by their bodies? Turn to page 13.

• Bird bills have adapted so that birds can eat particular types of food. To learn more go to pages 22–23.

• Some birds are carnivores, which means they eat meat. How do they catch their supper? See pages 36–39.

CRACKERS

Seeds can provide the main diet of birds. The strong, cone-shaped beak of the Purple Grenadier is perfect for cracking open seeds. This secretive bird searches for its food close to the ground, in the undergrowth and thickets.

STING OR BE STUNG

Many birds eat insects, but eating a bee could invite a painful sting. The European Bee-eater has learned a way to solve this problem. It holds the bee at the tip of its long beak and removes the stinger by rubbing it against a branch. It then squeezes the body of the bee to get rid of any poison before eating.

THE NECTAR OF LIFE

Hummingbirds, such as the Broad-billed Hummingbird, are very active. Each day they need to eat almost as much as their body weight in nectar—a sugary fuel—to keep up their strength. Hummingbirds can hover, which allows them to remain in one place while they insert their long bills into the trumpet-shaped flowers they visit. They can also fly backward, enabling them to back out of the flowers.

TOOL BIRD

The Woodpecker Finch of the Galápagos Islands is named for its habit of eating grubs that live in wood. But the finch, unlike woodpeckers, does not have a long tongue or a bill that is suitable for getting hold of the grubs. Instead, it uses a cactus spine or twig that is just the right shape to dig the grubs out.

HELPING HAND

The Yellow-billed Oxpecker, a relative of the starling, collects its food and helps other animals at the same time. The oxpecker feeds on the irritating ticks and lice that live in the skin and hair of giraffe, buffalo, antelope, and rhinoceros.

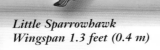

Little Sparrowhawk
Wingspan 1.3 feet (0.4 m)

Secretary Bird
6.6 feet (2 m)

Andean Condor
10 feet (3 m)

Mighty Hunters

THE HUNTING BIRDS are flying warriors. They are strong, fearless, and perfectly adapted to kill live creatures. The best hunters are the raptors, which include eagles, hawks, falcons, and owls. Their vision is up to three times better than that of humans. They can spot prey from a great distance. There is nothing pretty about what the raptors do. They grab and kill their victims with their needle-sharp claws called talons. They can also kill instantly with their strong, hooked bills, severing the neck with a single, mighty crunch. With their bills, they tear their kill into bite-size portions.

Kingfishers, herons, and storks are less dramatic, but they are equally skilled hunters. They hunt fishes, frogs, and other aquatic creatures. Sharp eyesight and lightning reflexes help them capture their slippery, fast-moving target. Storks are unusually quick. They can feel their prey in muddy waters and react with speeds that have been measured in thousandths of a second.

Some seabirds, such as the Great Skua, hunt other seabirds, along with the eggs and young of other birds. Skuas, giant-petrels, and albatrosses, like the land-based vultures, are often scavengers. In addition to hunting live prey, they eat carrion, the remains of dead animals.

GOTCHA!
The Azure Kingfisher is a clever hunter of fishes. It watches intently from a perch over water, then plunges bill-first to capture its prey.

INSIDE STORY

Game for a Sport

Falconry is an ancient sport that dates back many centuries. A falconer trains a falcon or hawk to capture prey, then fly back to its master with the kill. The master rewards the bird with food and keeps it in captivity until the next outing. Before the invention of accurate guns for hunting, falconry was popular for centuries. Falconers were among the first people to study birds seriously, learning their habits and skills. Today, only a small number of people continue the sport, and strict rules apply to protect the birds.

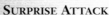

LETHAL WEAPONS
Many raptors hunt by day. They eat live prey that they catch with their strong feet. They are skilled hunters.

SURPRISE ATTACK
The African Pygmy Falcon uses its speed to surprise prey. It perches out in the open on dead trees, then suddenly pounces on its victim. This tiny falcon is about 8 inches (19 cm) long. It lives throughout the plains of eastern Africa, wherever the White-headed Buffalo-Weavers or Sociable Weavers are found. It uses these species' old nests for breeding.

HOOKED ON YOU
The beautiful Osprey hunts only fishes. The bird drops, feet first, into the water to grip a wriggling fish and carries it off for eating. The talons of the Osprey have special thorny growths called "spicules."

Word Builders

- The word **raptor** comes from the Latin word *raptare*, meaning "to seize and carry away."
- **Prey** is an animal killed for food by another animal. The word comes from the Latin *praeda*, meaning "booty," the food and valuables soldiers carry off when they conquer a territory.
- The name **Hamerkop** is an Afrikaans word meaning "hammerhead." This name refers to the shape of the bird's head when seen in profile.

That's Amazing!

- The two vulture species of North America hunt in different ways. The Turkey Vulture sniffs the air for the scent of carrion. The Black Vulture uses its keen eyesight. Sometimes Black Vultures wait for Turkey Vultures to pick up a scent and then follow them to the carcass.
- The Common Buzzard's territory extends 785 feet (240 m) above the ground. It will chase away any intruder that flies within this zone.

Pathfinder

- How do large raptors living in mountainous regions manage to fly so high and stay airborne for so long? The remarkable answer is on page 19.
- Birds that hunt during the night have developed special techniques for locating their prey. How do they do it? Fast-forward to pages 38–39.
- Some birds of prey, such as the Peregrine Falcon, have adapted well to life in the inner cities. Turn to pages 46–47 to find out more.

BORN TO RULE

In 1782, the Bald Eagle won the contest to become the national bird of the United States of America. Its fierce expression helped it triumph over the Wild Turkey, its rival for the honor. The Bald Eagle hunts mainly fishes and will sometimes take ducks or carrion. It will also steal food from other birds if it gets the chance.

STOP, THIEF!

The Antarctic Skua, like all skuas, has many ways of getting food. It often raids penguin colonies for both chicks and eggs, and also eats whatever carrion it can find. Most skuas will attack birds that have food to try to steal it from them.

FROGS' LEGS, ANYONE?

Hamerkops are small, storklike birds that live on the savannas of Africa, where they feed mainly on frogs. They also hunt fishes, shellfishes, and large insects. They build enormous stick-and-mud nests with small entrances in the forks of trees near their feeding grounds.

STOMPING GROUNDS

The Secretary Bird of the African savannas hunts snakes—even the venomous cobra—and other reptiles. Standing nearly 4.5 feet (1.3 m) tall, it stalks the grasslands, watching for signs of movement. The Secretary Bird's claws are weak and blunt. To make a kill, it stomps on its victim, breaking its neck.

CRUISE MISSILES

The Andean Condor travels great distances over the peaks of the Andes in South America looking for dead animals such as sheep and llamas. The Condor drops as soon as it spots a carcass. Unlike many other species, condors are prepared to share and rarely squabble with each other while feeding.

Oilbird | Feline Owlet-Nightjar | Kagu | Night Parrot

Night Raiders

IF YOU STEP outside on a moonless night, you have trouble seeing more than a few feet in front of you. But an owl's powerful night vision helps it detect a mouse moving far below on the forest floor. If the mouse makes the slightest rustle in the leaves, the owl can hear it, too. Some night birds, such as a cave-dwelling Oilbird, use echolocation—a way of using sound bouncing off objects—to find their way around in total darkness.

Birds that become active as darkness falls are called crepuscular (twilight active) or nocturnal (night active) birds. To protect them as they sleep during the day, owls, nightjars, and frogmouths have dull colored plumage that helps them fade into their surroundings. The green Night Parrot of Australia hides in the dense foliage of the saltbush. Most night birds, like the Kagu of New Caledonia, make spooky calls that can be heard over great distances.

There are advantages to birds hunting at night. The animals they prey on are more active in the dark. Most other birds are asleep, so they aren't competing with the night birds for food. Most bird predators are asleep as well.

NOW YOU SEE ME...
Like many night birds, the Tawny Frogmouth is very difficult to spot during the day. It is easily mistaken for a branch of the tree it perches on—unless it opens its large mouth.

...NOW YOU DON'T
The Common Potoo also adopts a pose like a stump of wood to make it hard to see during the day. It has a broad, flattened bill which is surrounded by a few bristles. These are used to funnel food into its mouth. Common Potoos use a swooping flight pattern to catch insects.

INSIDE STORY

Seeing in the Dark

Rose Ann Rowlett of the United States of America has been organizing birding expeditions worldwide for more than 20 years. She is skilled in locating birds that are seldom seen. Some live hidden in heavily forested regions, while others are shy and secretive or only come out at night.

To find night birds such as the Nocturnal Curassow in South America, or the Feline Owlet-Nightjar in New Guinea, Rowlett uses her knowledge of their habits, habitats, and sounds. She has a tape recorder with a sensitive microphone for recording sounds and a strong flashlight for illuminating the birds. Her work has led to exciting discoveries. In Panama, she and her colleagues made the first sound recording of the Crested Owl.

higher and larger ear opening | nostrils | eye socket | lower ear opening

70° binocular vision range

HUNTERS OF THE NIGHT
Many species of owls have ears that are asymmetrical. One is higher and larger than the other. This results in a slight difference in time between sound reaching each ear and helps owls judge the location of their prey with amazing accuracy.

110° field of vision range

Most birds' eyes are on the sides of their heads, but owls' eyes face forward. Their binocular vision—seeing an object with both eyes at the same time—helps them judge distance.

Word Builders

- Binocular vision is vision that uses both eyes at the same time. The word **binocular** comes from the Latin prefix *bi-*, meaning "two," and the Latin word *oculi*, meaning "eyes."
- **Crepuscular** birds come out during times of low light, such as dusk and dawn, or even when the sun is eclipsed. The word comes from the Latin root word *crepus*, meaning "dark," and the suffix *-culus*, which means "small."

That's Amazing!

- Barn Owls swallow their prey whole. After digesting the edible parts, they cough up a large pellet containing the fur, skull, and bigger bones. By dissecting these pellets, you can work out what an owl had for dinner.
- In one of its courtship rituals, the Common Nighthawk dives out of the sky and turns upward just before it hits the ground. At the bottom of the dive, wind rushing through its feathers makes a booming sound.

Pathfinder

- Cryptic coloration helps night birds hide during the day when they are resting. Do birds active during the day use plumage camouflage as well? The answer is on pages 16–17.
- The national bird of New Zealand is a nocturnal bird. Do you know its name? Go to page 20.
- Which nocturnal bird has mastered the art of hibernation? See page 61.

BURNING THE MIDNIGHT OIL

Is that a ghost in the night sky? No, it's just a Barn Owl out hunting. Hovering overhead, white underparts standing out against the darkness, Barn Owls are an eerie sight. And just as you recover from the shock of seeing one, chances are it will let out a shriek that makes your hair stand on end. Barn Owls are widespread throughout the world, living in open areas.

SUNSET WANDERINGS
Although the Black-crowned Night Heron is active during daylight hours, it usually waits until dusk to leave its roost and hunt for food. At this hour there is less competition from other heron species.

Owls swoop silently on their prey because their outer flight feathers have a serrated, or jagged, edge. This slows the flow of air over their wings, minimizing the noise they make as they flap. Most flying birds have smooth edges to their flight feathers.

Owls mostly hunt rodents. Once they have located their prey, they glide silently in for the kill. Raising their wings, they extend their sharp, curved talons to spike their target. A bite to the neck with their hooked bill finishes the job.

Bobolink

Arctic Tern

Rufous Hummingbird

Barn Swallow

Globetrotters

LIKE SOME PEOPLE, many birds have two homes—one for the summer and another for the winter. Flying makes it easy for them to travel from place to place. In the autumn they leave their summer nesting grounds and migrate to warmer places where they'll find more food. When the weather changes there, they migrate back again. Most birds migrate at precisely the same times every year. When the hours of sunlight get shorter in their nesting grounds, they know it's time to fly to warmer territory.

Some birds migrate in large flocks of one or more species, with first-time travelers and experienced birds flying together. Others, such as the Common Cuckoo, fly alone. When they meet other solitary travelers, they call back and forth. Small birds usually migrate at night because most of their predators are asleep and it is cooler, so flying is less tiring.

Birds are remarkable navigators. Some species orient their flight paths with the Sun, Moon, and stars. Others watch for large landmarks, such as mountain ranges or coastlines. Homing pigeons and a few other species have a tiny magnetic crystal in their heads. This may point toward Earth's magnetic pole, like a compass, allowing the birds to sense directions.

Not all birds migrate. About half the birds in the world remain close to one home for their whole lives.

INSIDE STORY

Screen Blips

As a teenager, Sidney Gauthreaux witnessed thousands of migrating birds, such as vireos, warblers, flycatchers, tanagers, and cuckoos, arriving exhausted and hungry in North America after crossing the Gulf of Mexico. From that time, he knew he wanted to study bird migrations.

In the 1950s, radar stations were being used to study the weather. These stations gave Gauthreaux a unique opportunity to track the movement of birds. Even the smallest of birds showed up on the screen. Gauthreaux now studies bird migration using a more powerful radar system called NEXRAD (Next Generation Radar). His research suggests that fewer birds are crossing the Gulf of Mexico today than in the 1960s. This may indicate that some bird populations are decreasing and may need protection.

Word Builders

• The word **migrate** comes from the Latin word *migrare*, which means "to change where one lives."
• The word **navigate** is from the Latin verb *navigare*, meaning "to sail."
• **Radar** tracks an object by measuring the time it takes for the echo of a radio wave to return from it. The word is the shortened form of the phrase *ra(dio) d(etecting) a(nd) r(anging)*.

That's Amazing!

• Dunlins, knots, and other small migrating birds have been seen at heights of over 21,000 feet (6,400 m). One pilot who was flying over the Outer Hebrides at 24,000 feet (7,300 m) saw a flock of migrating Whooper Swans sharing his air space.
• When a Manx Shearwater was taken from Britain to the United States and released, it found its way home—a trip of 3,200 miles (5,150 km) across the Atlantic Ocean—in only 12 days.

Pathfinder

• The words "lift," "vortex," and "updraft" are all connected with flight. To find out what they mean, turn to pages 18–19.
• Does flying come naturally to young birds? The answer is on pages 32–33.
• Some birds travel long distances on a daily basis, particularly seabirds when searching for food. How do they live over the oceans? See pages 48–49.

READING THE SIGNS
CELESTIAL BEACON
Experiments with nocturnal migrants, such as sparrows and warblers, showed that birds captured while migrating in the northern spring, and then placed in a planetarium, tried to fly in the direction of the North Star—no matter where that star was placed on the ceiling of the planetarium.

Latham's Snipe

Rufous Hummingbird

Bobolink

Barn Swallow

Far Eastern Curlew

Common Cuckoo

SUPER SKYWAYS
Huge numbers of migrating birds use a few main routes. They run along coastal areas and follow landmasses, avoiding long flights over water and high mountain ranges. The largest migrations are between North and South America, Eurasia and Africa, and East Asia and Australia. A few birds take other more difficult routes.

POLES APART
To test the theory that some birds navigate by the Earth's magnetic field, researchers attached a small magnet to the head of a pigeon. They found that the magnet caused the bird to lose its way. A piece of brass, with no magnetic force, had no effect on the pigeon's sense of direction.

FOLLOW THE LEADER
Some young birds learn the migration routes from their parents or other adult members of their species. Sandhill Cranes and Caspian Terns follow their parents from Canada to the south of the United States, calling to each other during the day and night.

LINING UP
Some aspects of bird behavior are a mystery to us. Flocks of Barnacle Geese, for example, fly in a V formation when they migrate to and from Greenland and Europe. Scientists are not sure why they and other species do this. Some believe the wings of the lead bird create swirling wind currents called vortices. These can cause updrafts of air, making flying easier for the bird behind. Other scientists think that birds fly in a V formation to see more clearly what is in front of them, and to avoid colliding with the birds ahead of them.

CHARTING THE LAND
Rivers, mountains, and coastlines seem to help birds migrating during daylight. Many of these landmarks run in a north-south direction, like the migration routes.

Where Birds Live

WHAT DO FORESTS, deserts, oceans, and cities have in common? They are all places where you will find birds. These, and many other environments, are called habitats. Where birds live affects the way they look and behave. Birds adapt to their habitats. Desert birds, for example, have clever ways to find water. Some city birds even nest on window ledges instead of cliffs. Turn the page and begin to explore some of the places that birds call home.

Camera   Telephoto lens   Binoculars   Tape recorder   Notebook

Bird Watching

YOU BELONG TO one of the biggest clubs in the world—a club you joined the first time you watched a robin on the lawn. Those who watch birds often call it birding. Some serious birders are amateur scientists, who do invaluable work that helps identify and protect birds. Some musicians are also birders. They are inspired by birdsong and calls. Artists and photographers are attracted to birds, too, because of the beautiful colors of their plumage. For all of us, birding can be a fascinating hobby, as simple or complex as we want it to be.

Dedicated birders often spend their weekends at wildlife refuges. They don't just watch birds. They record their sounds and try to identify different species. It takes practice to tell birds apart. Birders like to share their observations with others. Their findings can be useful to ornithologists in understanding birds and to conservationists who work to ensure that birds and their habitats are protected.

But remember, birds are shy around people. You'll have to stay still and quiet when you watch them.

The Rules of the Game

Going birding is fun and exciting, but there are a few rules that all birders should follow.

❶ Always use your common sense and behave in ways that do not endanger any birds, other wildlife, or people.

❷ Don't chase or flush birds. Stay away from nests and nesting colonies. You can watch and photograph birds without disturbing them.

❸ If you use tape recordings to attract birds, do not play them too often.

❹ Never handle birds or their eggs unless you are involved in recognized research work with qualified experts.

❺ Be sure to dress warmly because the best time to watch birds is in the cool morning or evening when birds are active.

INSIDE STORY

A World Without Song

In 1962, American biologist Rachel Carson published a book called *Silent Spring*. In it, she drew attention to the disappearance of many kinds of birds that were being poisoned by insecticides—chemicals used to kill insect pests. Describing the result, she wrote, "On the mornings that had once throbbed with the dawn chorus of robins, catbirds, doves, jays, wrens, and scores of other voices, there was now no sound; only silence lay over the fields and woods and marsh." When birds ate insects killed by the chemicals, the birds got sick or could not reproduce. Carson warned that such poisons can travel up the food chain and endanger many living things. Her book led to many international laws against the use of some insecticides and encouraged people to help protect the environment.

GOING, GOING ...
Many birds are under the threat of extinction. Some species have survived because scientists and birders kept a careful watch on their numbers and habitats.

WORKING TOGETHER
In 1986, a pair of Gurney's Pittas was found in Thailand. This species had not been seen since 1952. Then 30 more pairs were found. Today, farmers work with conservationists to protect the birds' forest habitat.

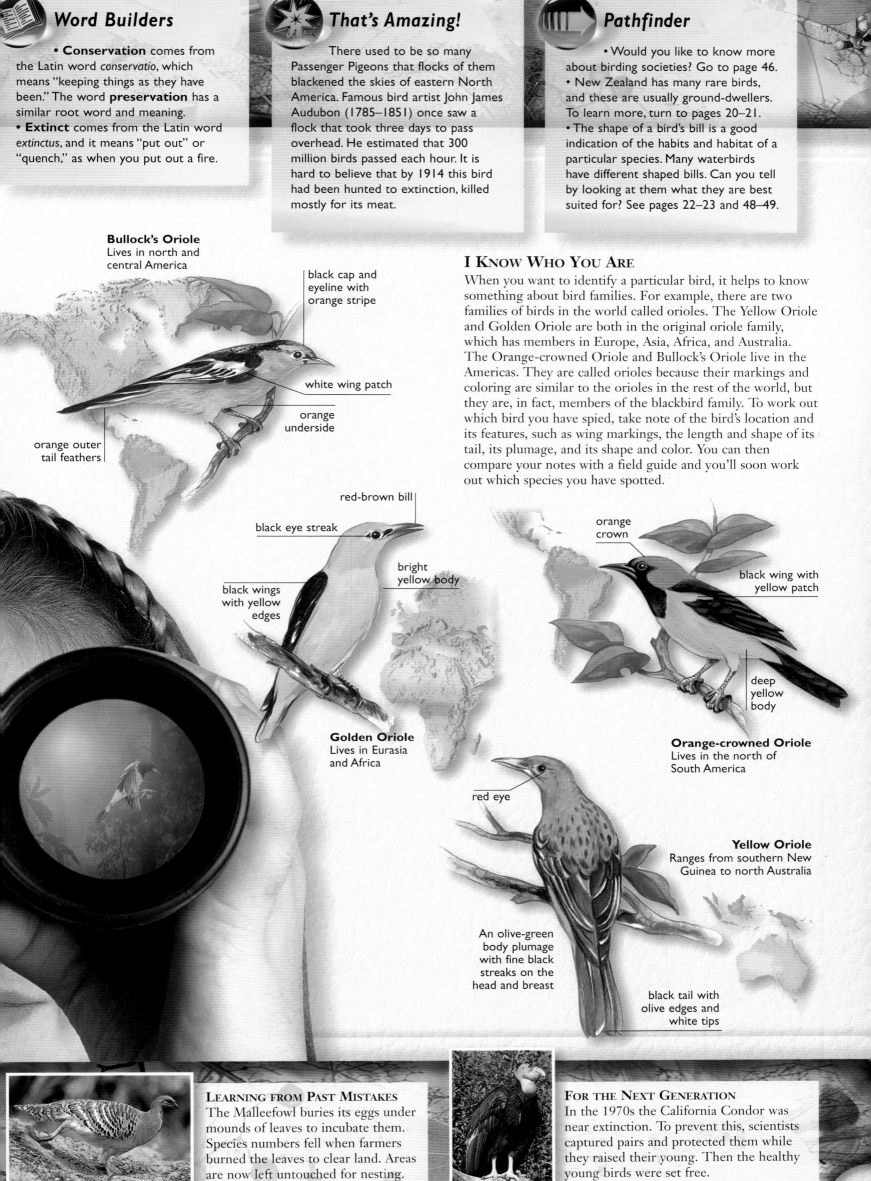

Word Builders

• **Conservation** comes from the Latin word *conservatio*, which means "keeping things as they have been." The word **preservation** has a similar root word and meaning.
• **Extinct** comes from the Latin word *extinctus*, and it means "put out" or "quench," as when you put out a fire.

That's Amazing!

There used to be so many Passenger Pigeons that flocks of them blackened the skies of eastern North America. Famous bird artist John James Audubon (1785–1851) once saw a flock that took three days to pass overhead. He estimated that 300 million birds passed each hour. It is hard to believe that by 1914 this bird had been hunted to extinction, killed mostly for its meat.

Pathfinder

• Would you like to know more about birding societies? Go to page 46.
• New Zealand has many rare birds, and these are usually ground-dwellers. To learn more, turn to pages 20–21.
• The shape of a bird's bill is a good indication of the habits and habitat of a particular species. Many waterbirds have different shaped bills. Can you tell by looking at them what they are best suited for? See pages 22–23 and 48–49.

Bullock's Oriole
Lives in north and central America

black cap and eyeline with orange stripe

white wing patch

orange underside

orange outer tail feathers

I KNOW WHO YOU ARE

When you want to identify a particular bird, it helps to know something about bird families. For example, there are two families of birds in the world called orioles. The Yellow Oriole and Golden Oriole are both in the original oriole family, which has members in Europe, Asia, Africa, and Australia. The Orange-crowned Oriole and Bullock's Oriole live in the Americas. They are called orioles because their markings and coloring are similar to the orioles in the rest of the world, but they are, in fact, members of the blackbird family. To work out which bird you have spied, take note of the bird's location and its features, such as wing markings, the length and shape of its tail, its plumage, and its shape and color. You can then compare your notes with a field guide and you'll soon work out which species you have spotted.

red-brown bill

black eye streak

bright yellow body

black wings with yellow edges

Golden Oriole
Lives in Eurasia and Africa

orange crown

black wing with yellow patch

deep yellow body

Orange-crowned Oriole
Lives in the north of South America

red eye

Yellow Oriole
Ranges from southern New Guinea to north Australia

An olive-green body plumage with fine black streaks on the head and breast

black tail with olive edges and white tips

LEARNING FROM PAST MISTAKES
The Malleefowl buries its eggs under mounds of leaves to incubate them. Species numbers fell when farmers burned the leaves to clear land. Areas are now left untouched for nesting.

FOR THE NEXT GENERATION
In the 1970s the California Condor was near extinction. To prevent this, scientists captured pairs and protected them while they raised their young. Then the healthy young birds were set free.

45

Barn Swallow

Black Kite

Black-billed Magpie

House Sparrow

City Slickers

IT TOOK BIRDS millions of years to adapt to their natural environments. So what happens when their natural world suddenly changes? Urban areas—cities and suburbs that are crammed with people, traffic, and buildings—have existed for only about 150 years. Birds haven't had much time to become accustomed to them.

Some birds couldn't adjust to city life, so they moved to other regions or died out. But many other birds are now at home in busy cities. You can find House Sparrows in cities in many parts of the world. The appearance of Barn Swallows, coming to make their nests in buildings, is a sign to some city dwellers that spring has arrived.

City birds have learned to take advantage of human behavior to make their lives easier. For example, sparrows and magpies congregate in parks and gardens because the soft soil makes it easy to catch worms. Others peck up crumbs spilled from office workers' lunches or are bold enough to eat straight out of people's hands. Black Kites scavenge scraps from garbage.

People who live in cities often try to make them as bird-friendly as possible. They put out birdbaths, bird feeders, and nesting boxes. In many places, areas of natural habitat have been saved from development so that birds can live and raise their young without harm. These areas, called bird refuges, are the homes of the greatest variety of birds.

CITY BOUND

New York City is the most heavily populated area in North America. But people are not the only ones attracted to the city. Central Park is in the center of New York. Almost 300 bird species have been spotted there. Some species live in the park all year, but most are migrating visitors. Birds seen there include Rock Doves, American Robins, Northern Mockingbirds, and Great Horned Owls. Peregrine Falcons can even be seen nesting on the ledges of the city's skyscrapers. These birds were introduced into the city in the 1960s. They were taught to use ledges because they were on the brink of extinction in their natural habitats, due to the use of pesticides.

Northern Mockingbird

Peregrine Falcon

Mallards

HANDS ON

Tracking Trends

In cities around the world, various programs keep track of where birds live. With your parents' help, you can find a program in your area. In North America there is a program called Project Feeder Watch. Thousands of people participate in this program by sending in reports about birds that visit bird feeders in their yards and gardens. Through efforts like these, scientists can monitor the health of different bird groups and can follow the northward expansion of species such as the Carolina Wren, Northern Mockingbird, Northern Cardinal, Tufted Titmouse, and Red-bellied Woodpecker. Counting birds is not as easy as you might think. If you see 15 chickadees in one hour, it doesn't automatically mean that 15 individuals have paid you a visit. Some of the 15 you counted may be birds that have stopped by twice or more in the hour.

Word Builders

- The Peregrine Falcon migrates from the Arctic to southern Europe, North America, and Asia. **Peregrine** comes from the Latin word *peregrinor,* meaning "to wander or travel."
- The word **urban** comes from the Latin word *urbs,* meaning "city" or "town." The Latin prefix *sub* means "beneath" or "below." The word **suburbs** means the outlying areas of a city.

That's Amazing!

- Legend has it that the city of Rome was saved in the early part of the first millennium by a flock of geese. The Goths of northern Europe were about to attack. The geese heard them coming, and honked so loudly that they woke the Roman soldiers.
- The Northern Mockingbird is a superb mimic. If it copies another bird's song, it can be impossible to tell which bird is doing the singing.

Pathfinder

- Do you know how to make a simple bird feeder? See page 34.
- What tools do birdwatchers need when they are in the field? Look at pages 44–45 to find out more.
- Gulls are seabirds that have adapted well to city life. If you would like to know more about seabirds, turn to pages 48–49.

Rock Doves

American Robin

Great Horned Owl

House Finches

THE HUMAN TOUCH

Cities are difficult places for birds to live, but people often help to make things easier for them.

TURNING OVER A NEW LEAF
Many woodland birds that have come to live in cities take advantage of the hard work of suburban gardeners. This European Robin is carefully inspecting freshly turned garden soil in search of worms.

OPERATION BIRD RESCUE
Birds face many dangers in cities, including collisions with cars and power lines and attacks from cats. Every day, wildlife services around the world come to the aid of many injured birds. This eagle is being prepared for an operation.

JUST GIVE A LITTLE WHISTLE
The White-faced Whistling-Duck is a naturally timid bird. In parks in Durban, South Africa, it has gradually gotten used to people and is happy to be fed by hand.

By the Sea

PERHAPS WE SHOULDN'T call our planet Earth, because more than seven-tenths of its surface is covered by water. Oceans and seas surround the land, and wherever there is seawater, there are places that attract birds: steep cliffs, tropical reefs, oceanic islands, mangrove swamps, and salt marshes. Birds flock to these habitats, attracted by plenty of food and moderate weather.

These birds have learned to gather their food in different ways. Plovers and sandpipers run along the water's edge in search of insects and shellfish buried in the sand. Gulls swoop down to scoop food off the surface of the water, while terns make shallow dives to catch fishes in the shallows. Blue-footed Boobies and Northern Gannets are also divers. Gannets sometimes dive from more than 100 feet (30 m) in the air to claim a fish from the water. Cormorants swim along the surface, diving from water level to browse along the coastal seabeds.

Shorebirds and seabirds have adapted well to their watery environments. The Hudsonian Godwit has a long, upwardly curved bill, ideal for probing deep into mud for food. As its name suggests, the Ruddy Turnstone turns over stones with its bill to get at the food underneath. The Black-necked Stilt has extremely long legs. It can wade into deep, still water without getting its body wet.

BEACH HOUSES

The shores of the Mediterranean Sea, enclosed between the south of Europe and the north of Africa, are lined with small evergreen shrubs, heathers, and scented herbs. These plants provide well-hidden nesting sites for many birds. Little Terns lay their eggs on the pebbles of the shore, where they are well camouflaged. The cliffs provide excellent nesting sites. On some of the sea's islands, there are huge colonies of Cory's Shearwaters. These birds nest in holes and cracks in the rocks. Many shearwater species are active at night at their nesting sites, and are seldom seen there during the day.

Northern Gannets

Little Tern

Little Tern

INSIDE STORY

Return Visitors

Ilsa Craig is an island off the coast of Scotland. It is a nesting site for Northern Gannets, and is the oldest known gannetry in the world. Researchers, under the guidance of Dr. Bernard Zonfrillo from the University of Glasgow, have been putting bands on the legs of Ilsa Craig's gannets for many years. Some of these banded birds have been spotted as far away as the Mediterranean Sea, a distance of more than 500 miles (800 km). But Dr. Zonfrillo has found that his gannets return to the island every year, and often nest in the same spot as they did in earlier years.

THE CALL OF THE OCEAN

LONE WANDERERS

Some birds live most of their lives far out at sea. Red-billed Tropicbirds roam, either alone or in pairs, over the oceans near the equator. They have long, pointed wings that help them fly quickly. Though these tropicbirds are good fliers, their short legs are set far back, making them very clumsy on land.

OCEAN FISHERS

Atlantic Puffins live in large colonies near the North Atlantic coasts. They find food out at sea, collecting fishes near the surface. Then they return to their nests to feed their young. Puffins can hold lots of fishes in their bills. The bills have backward-facing serrations, a bit like a comb's teeth.

Word Builders

- The word **booby** comes from the Spanish word *bobo*, which means "clown" or "stupid fellow." The Blue-footed Booby got its name from sailors who were amused by its clownish antics. The birds seem to fence each other with their bills.
- If something is difficult to see because of its color, it is described as having **cryptic** coloration. The word comes from the Latin word *crypta* and the Greek word *kryptos*, meaning "hidden."

That's Amazing!

- Razorbills, seabirds of the North Atlantic, look like penguins, but they can fly—most of the time. When a Razorbill molts each year, it loses all its flight feathers at the same time. So for about 45 days, until its new feathers grow in, it is as flightless as a penguin.
- Pelicans and cormorants have air sacs under their skin that enable them to float.

Pathfinder

- Which bird lives out over the ocean for most of the year, and has the largest wingspan of all birds? The answer is on pages 18–19.
- Which seabird is the fastest swimmer, even though it cannot fly? Turn to pages 20–21.

Cory's Shearwater

Black-bellied Plovers

Pied Avocets

Eurasian Curlew

Common Ringed Plovers

Yellow-legged Gull

Great Cormorants

PENGUINS OF THE NORTH
There are no penguins in the Northern Hemisphere, but Dovekies, which live in the Arctic, resemble penguins. They are black and white, and stand upright. Unlike penguins, Dovekies can fly.

SEA PIRATES
The Giant Petrel is a large, powerful bird that lives in the southern oceans. It is a scavenger. Scavengers eat dead fishes and other animals. Scavenging seabirds often follow fishing trawlers, ready to eat fishes caught in the nets, or garbage the crew throws overboard.

Purple Heron   *Saddle-billed Stork*   *Roseate Spoonbill*   *Japanese Crane*

Freshwater Homes

SWAMPS AND MARSHES are among the world's many different types of freshwater habitats. Rivers, creeks, lakes, and ponds are other expanses of fresh water. All are home to a great variety of birds. In the shallower waters, especially along the water's edge, dabbling ducks, such as the Mallard and teal, feed on plants and small aquatic animals. Deeper water is the territory of diving ducks and swans. Mud flats on the edge of these waterways provide shorebirds, such as yellowlegs, with worms, insects, and other invertebrates.

In all of these habitats you can see herons, egrets, ibis, and storks. These are wading birds with long legs and long bills. They can high-step through the water without getting their plumage wet. Herons and egrets use their long bills to stab fishes. Curlews and ibis have long, curved bills which they can stick in the mud to find tiny crabs and worms.

If you wanted to hide in these habitats, reed beds would be a good place to choose. Bitterns and rails hide from predators among grasses and reeds in such beds. Other birds live in marshlands, too. Wrens, sparrows, and blackbirds can sometimes be spotted nesting in trees that grow on dry hummocks.

Black Kites

Little Egrets

Magpie Geese

INSIDE STORY

Saving the Everglades

In 1947, an American named Marjorie Stoneman Douglas wrote a book called *The Everglades: River of Grass*. She described the beauty of this area of wetlands in southern Florida and warned of the damage that was being done to the freshwater environment as a result of real-estate developments and agricultural pollution. Most people at that time saw the Everglades as an unpleasant place full of alligators. But President Harry S. Truman was so moved by Douglas's words that he acted to protect the Everglades as a national park. Douglas supported the conservation of the Everglades until her death in 1998 at the age of 108. The United States government continues to help fund work aimed at reversing decades of damage to birds and other wildlife and their habitats. The Everglades is improving, but there is still much to do.

GONE FISHING
UNDER MY WING
When they fish, Black Herons spread their wings to reduce water reflections. This helps them to see fishes and may even attract smaller fishes into the shade.

WHAT'S UP?
The Cinnamon Teal is like all dabbling ducks. It almost never dives underwater for food. It feeds near the surface and reaches plants farther down by going tail up.

Word Builders

• The Black-necked Stork is Australia's only stork. It is known in that country as the **Jabiru**. This second name comes from the name Amazonian Indians gave to a South American stork.

• A **hummock** is a raised area, like a small hill. The word may come from an Old English word *humm*, which is related to the word "hump."

That's Amazing!

Anhingas are cormorant-like birds that live in freshwater wetlands in the Americas. They need to dive underwater to catch fishes. To help them do this, their feathers have tiny gaps that open to let the water in so they can sink, or close so they can float. When they want to fly, Anhingas must come out of the water and spread their wings to dry.

Pathfinder

• Which bird seems to run across water during courtship? Go to page 27.
• There are many ways for birds to catch slippery fishes. See pages 36–37 and 48–49 to find out more.
• A drink is always available to birds that live near fresh water. But where do ocean and desert birds find the moisture they need? For answers, turn to pages 48–49 and 60–61.

Black-necked Stork

Brolga

Comb-crested Jacana

Radjah Shelducks

PLAIN SAILING

Wetlands are rare in Australia. But the East and South Alligator rivers in the far north create vast lagoons at Kakadu, a national park covering nearly 1.6 million acres (645,000 ha). Kakadu is a birder's paradise. Its many types of habitats, such as mangrove forests, grass flood plains, and swamps, teem with more than a million water birds. You will often see great flocks flying overhead. The dry season runs from May to September. The floodwaters recede at this time, leaving only billabongs, or small ponds.

SCOOPING THE POOL

The lower part of the Black Skimmer's bill is longer than the upper part. The bird is able to fly with the lower part in the water, and when it feels a fish, it snaps its bill shut like a pair of scissors.

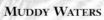

MUDDY WATERS

The Limpkin probes the water's edge with its long bill in search of food. It is fond of large snails, called apple snails, and other aquatic animals, such as crustaceans, frogs, freshwater clams, and insects.

51

Into the Woods

WOODLANDS ARE AS varied and as busy as the streets of a city. They seem peaceful enough, and you may think they all look much like one another. But look more closely and you'll find that each wooded area is a world of its own. Even within a single acre, there are many different trees and habitats supporting many different birds. Some species live on the lower levels of the forest and on the forest floor, while others dwell in the upper branches of the trees, finding many different sources of food.

In Europe and large parts of North America, the most common forest trees are maple, beech, and oak. These trees are all deciduous, which means they lose their leaves in the autumn. When new shoots sprout from their branches in spring, migrating birds start to return. They come for the rich supply of food, especially the insects. Woodland birds of prey also return. They know there will be many other birds on which they can prey. In the spring and summer, birds nest and rear their young in these woodlands.

In the autumn, before the trees shed their leaves, birds eat as much as they can to build up their stores of body fat. This fat becomes the fuel they will use as they make the long journey to warmer regions. Not all woodland birds migrate. For those that stay, food is scarce during winter, and they must search constantly for it. Sometimes, small groups of birds of different species roam together, each group looking in a different part of a tree for food.

European Robin

Eurasian Woodcock

HANDS ON

A Stroll in the Forest

Birds love trees. They are wonderful places in which they can hide, hunt for food, and nest. Because they are colored to blend into the woodland background, the birds can be difficult to see. This camouflage protects them from predators. The first sign of the bird may be its call. But if you know something about its shape, color, and habits, you are more likely to spot it.

Many birding clubs organize bird walks for beginners. You can learn a lot about identifying birds from the experts there and from other birders. You could also plan your own bird-finding mission. You'll need a field guide, binoculars, a journal, and a pen.

Field guides are books that have details of birds' appearances, habits, and habitats. Your local library or bookshop should stock them. Before you set out, make a list of the birds in the area you are planning to investigate. Keep this list handy when you go for your stroll. When you spot a bird, quickly draw it or write down its features in your journal for later reference. You never know—this first sighting may inspire a career in bird studies.

Word Builders

- The word **prothonotary** comes from the name of an important official in the Roman Catholic Church. The Prothonotary Warbler male's deep yellow color resembles the robes worn by the official on special days.
- The word **deciduous** comes from the Latin *decidere*, meaning "to fall from." The leaves of a deciduous tree fall off in the autumn.

That's Amazing!

The Ruffed Grouse performs a unique territorial display. This woodland bird perches on a hollow log and thumps its wings on its breast like Tarzan. The resulting sound is like a low-pitched drum beating faster and faster. The hollow log works to amplify the drumbeats. As this eerie sound reverberates through the forest, it tells other Ruffed Grouse males that this territory belongs to the thumper.

Pathfinder

- The Eurasian Sparrowhawk is a raptor, or bird of prey. To learn more about raptors, turn to pages 36–37.
- The Northern Mockingbird and the American Robin are woodland birds that can live in the city of New York. How have they and other birds adapted to city life? See pages 46–47.

SINGING FOR A LIVING

The bird calls and songs you can hear in the forest convey messages, just as human sounds and words do. Birds vocalize to signal danger, to identify other birds within their group, to defend their territories, or to court a mate.

WATER MUSIC

In the southern river woodlands of North America, the rich "sweet-sweet-sweet-sweet" song of the Prothonotary Warbler resounds throughout the swampy area.

FLUTE ORCHESTRA

The male Hermit Thrush begins its song with a crisp, clean note. It then sings in ascending and descending tones that sound like flutes playing in the distance. When migrating, these birds use their call to make sure they stay together.

LOVE SERENADES

As night falls, the male Nightingale sings to mark its territory and to charm a partner. Its sweet calls have inspired many love poems.

Winter Wren

Mistle Thrush

Eurasian Sparrowhawk

Blue Tit

WARNING CHIMES

If you hear a chorus of "twit-twit-twit" echoing through a woodland area, it may well belong to a group of Eurasian Nuthatches. These agile birds flit up and down tree trunks, warning one another of approaching danger.

HUNTING GROUNDS

An English forest is a deceptively tranquil place. One resident, the Eurasian Sparrowhawk, attacks small birds without warning. This sparrowhawk has short, rounded wings that allow it to twist and turn around the trees with great ease. The forest is a bit like an apartment block. Birds live on all levels. You might spy thrushes or woodcocks foraging for food on the ground, or wrens looking for insects in the understory, slightly above ground level. Blue Tits live in the upper levels, and robins in the mid-levels.

Great Tinamou   *Sunbittern*   *Hoatzin*   *Guianan Cock-of-the-Rock*

Deep in the Jungles

THERE ARE PLACES on Earth that may be home to species of birds that no one has ever seen. These remote places are the dense, tropical rain forests in Central and South America, southern Asia, northern Australia, and central and western Africa. They provide homes for almost half the life-forms on Earth. But they are rapidly disappearing because land is being cleared by timber companies and farmers.

Tropical rain forests have no spring, summer, autumn, or winter—it is either the wet or dry season. Because of this, rain forests are filled with lush, green trees that can grow as tall as 200 feet (60 m). The trees are often covered in brilliant swags of flowers. Birds, such as hawk-eagles, soar above their branches, and thick vines wind up their trunks. The top layer of the forest is called the canopy.

The closer you get to the ground, though, the darker it becomes. Shade-loving trees thrive in a level called the understory. In the dappled light and dense foliage, brightly colored birds, such as the trogons of South America, search for fruit and insects. But the sunlight can barely reach the small shrubs and leaf litter that carpet the forest floor. Here, thousands of insects scurry and flit about. They are easy pickings for birds, such as the Great Tinamou. Where there are creeks or rivers, Sunbitterns search for fishes.

TREE HOUSES

A vast array of tropical birds, such as the Harpy Eagle, lives high in the canopy of the Central and South American rain forests. This is an area of abundant light, warmth, and food. Birds, such as the Chestnut-eared Araçari, Chestnut-capped Puffbird, White-tipped Sicklebill, and Blue-crowned Trogon, also live among the trees. Some of these birds are brightly colored, but they can be difficult to spot among the green leaves and bright streaks of sunlight. Parrots, such as the Hyacinth Macaw, are perhaps the best known of rain forest birds.

Hyacinth Macaw

INSIDE STORY

Surrounded by Sound

Ted Parker (1953–93) worked for Conservation International. He recorded birds around the world, and gradually learned the songs and calls of over 4,000 species—more than any other person in history. But he is most noted for his work in the rain forest and mountain habitats of South America. Here, more than one-third of all bird species live in a region that is only one-sixth of the Earth's landmass. Parker discovered many species in these dense, remote locations that no one knew existed. By the 1980s, he became concerned about the effect that the loss of habitats was having on wildlife. His studies into this area enabled scientists and governments to determine which habitats and bird species needed urgent protection.

A WAKE-UP CALL FROM THE WILD

Every day, around the world, 214,000 acres (87,000 ha) of rain forest are destroyed. This is almost the same size as New York City in the U.S.A. Once a forest is cleared, the birds and other wildlife lose their habitats and may even become extinct. Because most of these rain forests are so dense, it is likely that some animals will die out before scientists have had a chance to discover them. To help prevent this situation from getting worse, some countries have set aside pockets of rain forest as reserves. This may help save some tropical birds and wildlife from extinction.

PLOWING AFRICA

The largest of the turaco species, the shy Great Blue Turaco, lives in western and central Africa. The rain forests in these regions have been cut down in order to create farmlands to feed the almost one billion people who live in Africa.

Word Builders

• The word **jungle** makes you think of a dense, lush, tropical forest. But it comes from the Sanskrit word *jangala*, which means desert.

• **Hoatzin** is a Nahuatl word. Nahuatl was spoken by the Aztecs of Mexico and Central America. This language has given us words such as coyote and chocolate.

• A **canopy** is a rooflike covering. The word comes from the Greek *konopeion*, meaning "mosquito net."

That's Amazing!

• When displaying, a Guianan Cock-of-the-Rock is quite a sight. It extends its crest forward so that it completely covers its bill, and narrows its round eyes to become slits.

• Because of the downward curve of its bill, the White-tipped Sicklebill is a hummingbird that has trouble hovering. To feed from tubular flowers, it has to use its strong feet to clamber over the flowerheads.

Pathfinder

• Do you know what a young Hoatzin looks like? Go to page 11.

• Birds of Paradise are among the most colorful and fascinating birds on Earth. They live in the rain forests of New Guinea and northern Australia. To learn more, see pages 16–17.

• Which South American rain forest bird has a very large bill that has made it famous worldwide? Turn to pages 22–23 to find out.

Chestnut-eared Araçari

Chestnut-capped Puffbird

Harpy Eagle

White-tipped Sicklebill

Blue-crowned Trogon

MADAGASCAR MARVEL
Almost half of Africa's Madagascar Island birds are threatened with habitat loss. The Sunbird Asity is only one of a few birds that can adapt to life after logging. It can live in new growth forests.

HANGING ON
The Blue-crowned Hanging-Parrot lives in Malaya, Sumatra, and Borneo. Forests there have existed in their present form for 70–100 million years. If these ecosystems are destroyed, they can never be recreated.

FIGHTING CHANCE
The Double-wattled Cassowary is a flightless bird that lives in New Guinea and northern Australia. Its habitat in Australia is a World Heritage site, which helps protect the birds.

Wide Open Spaces

GRASSLANDS HAVE DIFFERENT names in different parts of the world. They are known as savannas, prairies, pampas, and steppes. They can be harsh habitats, occurring where climates are too dry and soils too poor for trees to grow.

On the enormous African savannas, Ostriches and White-quilled Bustards feed on plants and insects. Hungry vultures circle in the sky, waiting for lions to leave their kill. And many other birds, including sandgrouse and a variety of brilliantly colored finches, feast on the largest food supply of this region—grass seeds.

In South America there are the vast, rolling pampas, where the Rufous Hornero builds its strange mud nests. But in North America and Europe there are few unspoiled grasslands. Much of the land has been taken over for farming. These large farms and other human developments have taken away the nesting areas and natural food sources of many birds, causing some to be in danger of extinction. The Greater Prairie-Chickens that still survive have learned to eat the grain in farm fields, especially after heavy snowfall, and some farmers consider them a pest.

The Russian steppes, which stretch into northern Asia, are cooler in temperature than most grasslands because they lie farther from the equator. The nights here can be freezing cold. The Rosy Starling eats almost anything it can find. It has adapted to the treeless habitat by wedging its nests in cracks in rocky outcrops.

MAKING A BEELINE

All animals must be resourceful in order to survive the harsh conditions of the African savannas. The Greater Honeyguide eats insects like many other birds but is unique in its ability to digest beeswax. To get the wax, the honeyguide leads a honeybadger, mongoose, or even a person to a beehive, catching their attention with its chattering calls and repeated spurts of flight. The honeyguide waits for the nest to be opened by the honey seeker, and then seizes its chance to feed on the beeswax.

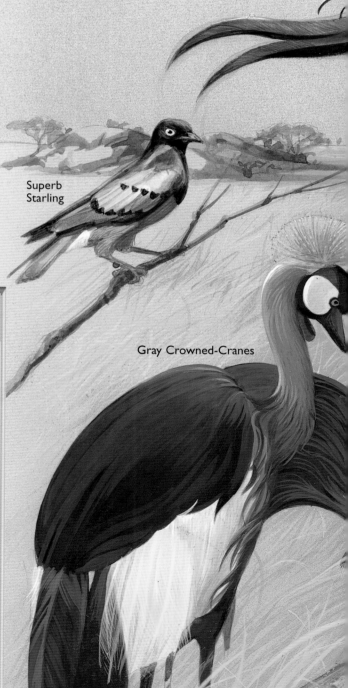

Superb Starling

Gray Crowned-Cranes

HANDS ON

A Place to Hide

Birds will come near you only if they think you're not there. You need to sit still and quiet, and out of sight, perhaps behind some bushes or a fence. In open spaces like grasslands, a blind can provide an ideal place from which to secretly observe birds.

❶ You'll need four sturdy poles, about 6 feet (1.8 m) long, string, one or two pieces of dark cloth, about the size of a double-bed sheet or larger, and some clothespins.

❷ Arrange your poles. Some people shape them like a tepee, tying the poles together at the top with string. Others prefer a box-shape, with the poles pushed firmly into the ground to keep them upright.

❸ Wrap your cloth around the poles, and secure with clothespins.

❹ Fold the cloth so that you create an entrance to your blind. On the opposite side, make a small observation window at eye level. Then wait patiently for the birds.

Word Builders

- The word **savanna** comes from the extinct Taino language. It was spoken by the Arawaks, people who lived on the islands of the Caribbean. Their word for grassland was *zabana*.
- The **Rufous Hornero** builds a nest that resembles a bread oven, hence the bird's name. The Spanish word for baker is *hornero*. Rufous comes from the Latin word *rufus,* meaning "red."

That's Amazing!

- The Red-billed Quelea lives on the plains of Africa. It gathers in roosts that number tens of millions of birds. These birds feed on grain and can strip a farmer's large crop in one day.
- The Burrowing Owls of North and South America have gone underground to nest and keep safe from predators. They live in the old burrows of prairie dogs or other mammals, emerging at night to feed.

Pathfinder

- If you want to know more about flightless grassland birds, such as rheas, check out pages 20–21.
- To see the strange mud nest that the Rufous Hornero builds, and many other nests, turn to pages 28–29.
- Which grassland bird hops on the back of antelope, giraffe, buffalo, and rhino when it is looking for something tasty to eat? See page 35.

IF THE BILL FITS

The bills of most seed-eating birds are shaped like a cone, and are usually short and stout. This shape enables the birds to exert pressure and crack the outer layer of the seeds to get at the nutritious contents. The grasslands of South America are home to a large number of seed-eating birds.

Paradise Whydah

Greater Honeyguide

Ostriches

Helmeted Guinea-Fowl

The Double-collared Seedeater's bill has a curved culmen, or upper ridge. This bill adaptation is perfectly suited for opening the seeds of a great variety of grasses and small plants.

The Great Pampa-Finch has a heavy, curved bill that copes well with the large seeds of the huge grasses that grow on many parts of the Pampas of Argentina.

The striking Red-crested Cardinal has a bill that is capable of husking a large variety of seeds. This bird can usually be seen feeding in pairs or small groups.

57

Rufous Rockjumper

Mountain Chickadee

Snow Finch

Alpine Accentor

On Higher Ground

MOST OF THE WORLD'S continents have their own great mountain range—the Rockies, Appalachians, and Andes in America, the Alps, Pyrenees, and Urals in Europe, and the mighty Himalayas in Asia. As you travel up a mountain, the temperature falls. This creates a vast range of habitats, allowing many bird species to find food and nesting sites.

At the base, forests tend to grow thickly. Many birds in North America and Europe feed on seeds from cold-forest trees known as conifers—pines, spruces, cedars, and firs. Depending on the season, some birds migrate between these forests and the meadows higher up. Mountain Chickadees and Alpine Accentors forage in the forests during the cooler months but travel above the tree-line in search of insects when it is warmer. The occasional bush and conifer on the meadows provide year-round shelter for birds such as the Snow Finch.

The meadows give way to rocky outcrops and steep cliffs. Rufous Rockjumpers build nests in the crevices lower down, but few birds live in the windswept heights. If they do, they need to defend large territories because food is scarce. Andean Condors search for many hours over vast areas before they find carrion on which to feed.

Spotted Forktail

INSIDE STORY

A Journey of Discovery

In 1803, United States president Thomas Jefferson planned a trip of exploration to find an overland route from the Mississippi River to the Pacific Ocean. Meriwether Lewis and William Clark were the leaders of the expedition, which set out in the spring of 1804. Along the way, they were helped by a young Shoshoni guide named Sacagawea.

Two years later, the expedition returned to the Mississippi with tales of amazing adventures and descriptions of mountain birds and wildlife that Easterners had never seen. Lewis was a keen observer of the newly found birds and brought back many sketches he had made of them. Two of the bird species were eventually named for the explorers—Clark's Nutcracker and Lewis's Woodpecker.

SUMMER RETREATS

Coniferous forests surround the base of mountains in temperate zones. The Japanese Waxwing of north Asia comes to these forests for fruit. These birds have waxlike droplets on the tip of some of their wing feathers, which explains their name.

The Steller's Jay lives in the Rocky Mountains. It is a very noisy bird. Sometimes it sounds like a hawk screeching while at other times it sings sweetly. The Steller's Jay likes stealing food from picnics.

Word Builders

• The word **condor** comes from the Quechua word *kuntur*. Quechua is a language of Indians who live in the South American Andes.
• The Indian Hill Myna has a syrinx, a specialized organ at the base of the windpipe, that allows it to mimic human speech so well that it's hard to tell the bird from the person. **Myna** comes from the Hindi word *maina*, which is the ancient name for this bird.

That's Amazing!

Some birds, such as the small Mountain Chickadees, survive dramatic drops in high-altitude temperatures by decreasing their body temperature by as much as 50 degrees Fahrenheit (10 degrees C). They do this by lowering their metabolism, breathing rate, and heart rate. This puts them into a state of inactivity that is known as torpor.

Pathfinder

• Which bird of prey can be found gliding high over the Himalayas? Turn to page 9 to find out.
• What sort of nests do birds build on mountain cliffs? See page 29.
• Coniferous forests stretch across the top of the Northern Hemisphere. Which type of forest lies near the equator, and how do birds live in that habitat? Pages 54–55 will reveal all.

Red-billed Magpie

Indian Hill Myna

Blue Whistling Thrushes

Wallcreeper

Himalayan Monals

PHEASANT LIFE

The Himalayas are the world's highest mountains. Many birds live on the slopes, including the Blue Whistling Thrush, Wallcreeper, Red-billed Magpie, Indian Hill Myna, and Spotted Forktail. Himalayan Monals live in the forests and meadows about halfway up. These ground-dwellers use their curved bills to dig up roots, bulbs, and insect grubs, often from snow-covered soil. When in danger, they run down the slopes, flapping their wings for speed. Then, when the scare is over, they waddle slowly back up to their feeding grounds.

Treecreepers do as their name suggests—they creep up the tree trunks. They climb in a spiral motion, probing the bark with their curved bills for insects and larvae. When they reach the top, they fly to the base of the next tree and start again.

The Red Crossbill has a bill that crosses at the tip. This shape, along with the birds' strong muscles, helps the crossbill to pry open fresh pine cones and get at the seeds inside. Other birds have to wait for the cones to open naturally.

Lichtenstein's Sandgrouse

Houbara Bustard

Harris's Hawk

Gibber Chat

Fire and Ice

THE HARSHEST ENVIRONMENTS on Earth are the superhot deserts and the ice-capped Arctic and Antarctic regions—the North and South poles. The ground is either baked hard or frozen solid. Few plants or animals can live in these bleak habitats, so birds (and other creatures) must find clever ways to survive.

In the African deserts, the male Lichtenstein's Sandgrouse uses its belly feathers like a sponge. It lies in whatever water it can find and soaks its feathers. Then it carries the liquid back to its young. The Houbara Bustard lives in the wide arid belt between Algeria and central Asia, and gets the water it needs from water-filled insects and plants. Harris's Hawks nest among the spikes of cacti. They help each other to survive by hunting for prey in groups. The Gibber Chat, in the stony deserts of Australia, raises no young when conditions are too harsh.

Desert birds conserve energy by staying quiet during the heat of the day. The best time to see them is at sunrise or sunset, when the temperatures are cooler.

The polar regions are the coldest places on Earth. Huge ice sheets grow larger in winter, and shrink in summer. Most birds visit these regions in summer only, when the weather is milder and there is more food to eat. But the Adélie Penguin and the Emperor Penguin are hardy enough to live in Antarctica all year.

PRICKLY SITUATIONS

Cacti are plants with scales or spikes that people avoid touching. But in North America's western deserts, birds use these plants to help them survive. The Verdin hangs upside down from cactus branches while it looks for insects. The Gila Woodpecker makes two kinds of holes in the saguaro cactus. One is for hunting for insects; the other is a nest hole, in which it lays its eggs. Elf Owls use abandoned Gila Woodpecker holes for shelter and nesting. The Gambel's Quail lives among the cacti, feeding mostly on seeds and the occasional insect.

Cactus Wren

INSIDE STORY

Doing It the Hard Way

Because Emperor Penguins live in Antarctica, little was known about their nesting habits until the early 1900s. Three explorers—Edward Wilson, Apsley Cherry-Garrard, and Henry Bowers—made a harrowing climb around the edge of the Ross Ice Shelf in the winter of 1911. They climbed down a steep, icy ridge, and were amazed to discover a rookery—the place where penguins incubate their eggs and care for the hatchlings.

Hundreds of male Emperor Penguins were gathered in the cold, bleak weather. Each penguin had a single large egg resting on its feet. The egg was covered by a special flap of skin that kept it warm even when the temperature fell as low as -80 degrees Fahrenheit (-60 degrees C). Later, it was discovered that female Emperor Penguins, after having laid their eggs, spend the winter in the sea, leaving the males to hatch the eggs. They return later to help rear the young.

Word Builders

- The arid gibber plains of Australia are covered in weather-worn rocks and boulders. **Gibber** comes from the Australian Aboriginal Dharug word *giba*, meaning "stone."
- **Tundra** comes from a Russian word that means "marshy plain."
- **Arctic** is from the Greek word *arktikos*, meaning "bear." The northern constellation called the Great Bear can be seen above the Arctic.

That's Amazing!

- The Poorwill lives in the western deserts of North America. It is the Sleeping Beauty of the bird world. The only bird known to hibernate for long periods in winter, it sleeps so deeply that it doesn't wake even when someone picks it up and holds it.
- The Rock Ptarmigan flies into soft snowbanks to sleep. It can sleep safely, insulated by the snow, because it has left no tracks for predators to see.

Pathfinder

- The Persian Gulf in the Middle East is surrounded by hot, burning sands. One bird has found a clever way to keep its eggs cool there. See page 9.
- Which seabird steals into penguin colonies to take their eggs for supper? The answer is on page 37.

Verdin

Elf Owl

Gila Woodpecker

Roadrunner

Gambel's Quail

SUMMER HOMES

Vast treeless plains around the Arctic are called tundra. Some birds live there all year, but most come only during the summer.

CHANGING COLORS

The Rock Ptarmigan lives all year on the tundra. During summer, the brownish color of its plumage blends in with the rocks and lichens of its habitat. The ptarmigan molts during fall, turning white to match the winter snow.

NURTURING MALE

The Red-necked Phalarope lives in the Arctic during the warmer summer months. The female is more brightly colored than the male. She takes the lead in courtship rituals. The male incubates the eggs and takes care of the chicks.

SKILLFUL HUNTER

The Snowy Owl may kill up to 10 lemmings a day. When plenty of food is available, the females raise many chicks. When food is scarce, they hatch no young.

SUMMER MIGRANT

Lapland Longspurs migrate to the tundra to nest in summer. Because there are no trees, the male must hop up onto rocks when displaying or defending his territory.

bill *clutch* *crest* *display* *egg tooth*

Glossary

adaptation A change in a bird's or other animal's body that allows it to function and reproduce more successfully in a particular environment.

altricial Helpless at birth or hatching, and dependent on care from adults. Many bird hatchlings are altricial.

bill The horny covering of the jaws of a bird, comprising two halves—the maxilla and the mandible. Sometimes called a beak.

brood A number of young birds hatched in one clutch or group. As a verb, "to brood" means to shelter young birds from the sun, heat, or cold.

call A sound, other than a song, used by birds for communicating messages.

carrion The flesh of dead animals that is eaten by birds or other animals. Creatures that eat carrion are called scavengers.

class One of several divisions into which scientists divide animals. Birds are in a class of their own, which is called Aves.

clutch All the eggs laid by a bird in one breeding cycle.

conifer A tree or shrub, such as a pine, fir, or spruce, that produces cones.

conservation An effort by people to protect a natural area so that plants and animals can live there undisturbed by human development.

courtship The behavior patterns that male and female birds and other animals display when they are trying to attract a mate.

crepuscular Active at dusk or dawn, when the light level is low.

crest The elongated or erect feathers of a bird's crown.

cryptic The kind of marking or coloring that makes a bird difficult for a predator to see against the bird's natural surroundings.

deciduous A description of a tree that loses all its leaves at once, usually in the autumn. Maples, oaks, and birches are deciduous.

display A behavior or set of behaviors that aims to attract the attention of another bird. Also, it may threaten or distract another bird or animal.

distribution Where a species is found, including its habitat, range, and location at different seasons.

diurnal Active during the daytime.

ecosystem The carefully balanced interaction of plants, animals, and their environment, usually in a particular habitat.

egg The large, rounded shell that contains a yolk and a white, laid by a female bird. If it has been fertilized, the egg contains a tiny embryo that will grow into a baby bird, using the yolk and white as food. When mature, the baby will break out of the eggshell.

egg tooth A sharp, tooth-shaped calcium deposit that grows on the tip of the bill of an embryonic bird. The bird uses the tooth to help it break through the shell when it is hatching.

endemic Found only in one habitat or region. Most penguins are endemic to the cold waters of the Southern Hemisphere.

environment The whole of an animal's surroundings, which influences the animal's development and behavior.

evolution The constant genetic adaptation of species to their environments.

extinct No longer existing alive anywhere in the world. Many bird species are extinct.

feather One of the objects that make up a bird's covering or plumage. A feather is made of a horny substance called keratin, and has a long shaft to which two vanes are attached. The vanes, made up of many closely spaced barbs, give the feather its shape and color. Feathers have many uses. They keep birds warm and dry, and help them to fly.

field mark A particular feature of a bird species that helps birdwatchers tell it apart from other species.

fledgling A very young bird that has left the nest in which it hatched. Prior to leaving the nest, it is known as a nestling.

habitat The native or natural environment of a bird, other animal, or plant.

hatch To break free from the eggshell.

imprinting A process in which hatchlings or other very young animals attach themselves to a parental figure.

incubation Keeping eggs warm so that the embryos inside will grow and hatch. The parent bird usually uses its body to warm the eggs, but some birds use sand or rotting leaves and plants.

instinct An inborn (or innate) behavior that develops in a bird or other animal without learning. Ducklings begin to swim by instinct.

invertebrate An animal that does not have a backbone, such as a worm, crab, or jellyfish.

iridescent Showing different colors as light strikes from different angles, like a soap bubble or oil on a pool of water. The plumage of some birds is iridescent.

juvenile A young bird or other animal. Some juveniles have markings that are very different from those of adults of the same species, so they may be difficult to identify.

feather *fledgling* *invertebrate* *juvenile*

molting *nest* *predator* *shaft*

mandible The lower part of a bird's bill, usually a bit smaller than the upper part.

mate A bird's partner during courtship and mating.

maxilla The top part of a bird's bill, usually a bit larger than the lower part.

migration The movement of birds from one place to another, which usually occurs in the spring and autumn.

mobbing An action used by a flock of small birds to drive away a predator. They follow, surround, and attack the larger bird, which often flies away. The flock may also use mobbing to teach young birds which predators to be wary of.

molting The process by which birds shed old, worn feathers and replace them with new ones.

nectar The sweet, sugary secretions of flowering plants that attract birds and insects.

nest A pocketlike structure that is often made of branches, twigs, and grass. Many birds build nests in which to lay and incubate their eggs, and to feed their young.

nestling A young bird that has not yet left its nest after hatching. It relies on its parents for food and protection.

nocturnal Active at night.

ornithologist A person who makes a scientific study of birds.

pellet A small, hard object that some birds regurgitate (spit up) containing parts of their food that they could not digest, such as bones, fur, or shell.

pigment Any substance that creates color in the skin, feathers, or tissues of a bird, other animal, or plant.

pouch A sac-like area of skin stretched between the two sides of the lower jaw of a bird, such as the one on a pelican.

predator A creature that hunts and eats other live creatures. Birds of prey are predators that hunt other birds or mammals.

preen For a bird, to clean and restore the structure of its feathers so that they remain in good condition.

prey An animal that is killed by another animal to be eaten. The killer animal is called a predator.

range The entire geographic area across which a species is regularly found.

rectrix A technical term used by scientists to describe a bird's tail feathers.

remige A technical term used by scientists to describe a bird's flight feathers.

roost An area where birds come to socialize, preen, or sleep.

scavenger A bird or other animal that feeds on dead animals. Many vultures and crows are scavengers.

scrape A depression in the ground made by some bird species in which to lay their eggs.

shaft The long, slender, central part of the feather that holds the vanes.

solitary A bird that stays by itself at least during some seasons of the year.

song A sound or series of sounds made by a bird to announce its territory or seek a mate. Bird songs can be simple or elaborate, and some are very musical.

species A group of birds, other animals, or plants with common features that distinguish them from any other group.

sternum The breastbone. Flying birds have a large, deeply keeled sternum to anchor their powerful flight muscles.

tapered Becoming smaller or thinner toward one end.

territory An area that is defended by a bird or other animal species against other creatures of the same species, especially during the mating season.

thermal A column of warm air that is rising. Some birds ride upward in thermals, to gain height, then glide slowly downward again.

theropods A group that includes all meat-eating dinosaurs.

torpor A state of dormancy—a kind of sleep—in which a bird or other animal can lower its heart rate and body temperature to save energy, especially during the night or periods of cold temperatures.

tundra The vast, treeless Arctic plains of northern Asia, Europe, and North America.

vane The part of the feather that grows from the central shaft.

vertebrates Animals with backbones, including birds, fishes, reptiles, amphibians, and mammals. The vertebrae are the bones that make up the spine.

vortex Circular air currents made by the movement of the wingtips of a bird.

yolk The yellow part of an egg. If the egg is fertilized, a tiny embryo grows inside the egg, using the yolk (and the white) as food.

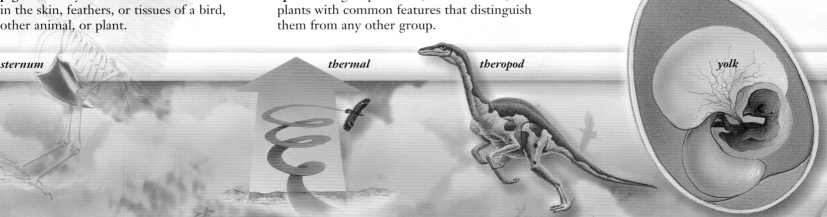

sternum *thermal* *theropod* *yolk*

Index

The publishers would like to thank the following people for their assistance in the preparation of this book: Barbara Bakowski, Renee Clark, Sidney A. Gauthreaux, Matthew Hoffman.
Our special thanks to the following children who feature in the photographs: Sienna Berney, Michelle Burk, Simon Burk, Julia Eger, Matthew Eger, Kevin Peters, Andrew Tout.
PICTURE CREDITS (t=top, b=bottom, r=right, l=left, c=center, e=extreme, f=flap, F=front, C=cover, B=back)
Ad-Libitum 5b, 12bl, 12bc, 22bl, 22bc, 25tr, 28bl, 30c, 30bl, 34c, 34tr, 42tr, 43tr, 44/45c, 44t, 52b, 56bl (M. Kaniewski). **AKG Photo London** 10tr, 18c, 18cl. **AP/Wide World Photos**, 50cl (Kathy Willens). **Aquila Wildlife Images** 11br (J. J. Brooks), 34bc (Gary Smith), 50bl (M. C. Wilkes). **ARDEA London** 55bc, 59br (D. Avon), 57br (F. Collet), 61cr (J. Daniels), 57cr (John S. Dunning), 28c (M. D. England), 15br, 44bc (Kenneth Fink), 38tr (Peter Steyn), 61tr. **Auscape** 47cr (John Cancalosi), 21tr, 49br (Jean-Paul Ferrero), 21cr (Ferrero-Labat), 38br, 45br (François Gohier), 14br (Mark Hamblin-OSF), 61br (Owen Newman-OSF). **BBC Natural History Unit** 16br (Richard Kirby), 49bl (Steve Packham), 61ebr (Tom Vezo). **Bruce Coleman Collection** 47br (Trevor Barrett), 45bl (John Cancalosi), 17b (Brian J. Coates), 39cr (Rita Meyer), 19cl, 46bl (Kim Taylor), 28bl (Gunter Ziesler). **Clemson University, SC** 40tr (C. G. Belsu). **CSIRO Australia, Division of Wildlife and Ecology** 20c (David Westcott). **Frank Lane Picture Agency** 19cr (H. D. Brandl), 34bl (Hugh Clark), 35br (F. Hartmann), 47tr (J. Hawkins), 51br (David Hosking), 36bl, 54br, 59bl (E & D Hosking), 37br (Philip Perry Kruger), 51bl (Fritz Polking), 58br (Leonard Lee Rue), 35tr, 53br, 53cr (Roger Wilsmhurst), 27br (Martin Withers). **Magnum Photos** 44bl (Erich Hartmann).
Marie Read Natural History Photography 27tr. **Minden Pictures** 37tr (Frans Lanting). **National Geographic Society** 11bl (O. Louis Mazzatenta). **Natural History Photographic Agency** 57cr (Bill Coster). **National Museum of Natural History** 15bl (Smithsonian Institution/Chip Clark). **Oxford Scientific Films** 48bl (Mike Birkhead), 10br (David M. Dennis), 58bl (Mark Hamblin), 26l (Mark Jones), 35bl (Dr. F. Koster), 22cr (John Netherton), 32bl

(James H. Robinson), 35tl (Tony Tilford), 55br (Steve Turner), 34br (Tom Ulrich). **Photo Researchers Inc.** 53ecr (Bill Dyer), 53tr (Brock May), 44/45c (Anthony Mercieca). **Jan Pierson** 38c. **Planet Earth Pictures** 15bl (Mary Clay), 22tr (Geoff du Feu), 36c (Paulo de Oliveira), 55bl (Pete Oxford). **Popperfoto** 61c. **Wendy Shattil/Bob Rozinski** 32c. **The Granger Collection** 58c. **The Photo Library, Sydney** 12bc (Eye of Science/SPL), 21br (Nick Green), 32cl (Herbert Lange). **Tom Stack and Associates** 48br (John Gerlack), 16bl (Larry Tackett). **Twin Tigers Photography** 9bl (Graeme Outerbridge). **Ullstein Bilderdienst** 33b (dpa). **University of Glasgow** 48c (Dr. Bernard Zonfrillo). **VIREO/Academy of Natural Sciences** 50br (A. Morris).
ILLUSTRATION CREDITS
Jane Beatson 4crt, 25tl, 36t, 36b, 37b, 43tl, 52/53c, 52t, 54/55c, 54t, 63tcr. **David Blundell/Wildlife Art Ltd.** 25b (Globes), 41t, 41r, 41c (Globes). **Dan Cole/Wildlife Art Ltd.** 5c, 6tr, 8/9c, 8t, 9r, 24br, 25b (Birds) 26/27c, 26b, 27b, 26t, 40/41b, 41br, 41cr, 40t, 41t (Birds), 62tcr. **Barry Croucher/Wildlife Art Ltd.** 4tr, 6c, 7c, 10/11c, 10t, 11cl, 11c, 11cr, 18/19c, 18t, 18cr, 18b, 19b, 63bcl, 63bcr. **Christer Eriksson** 36/37c. **Lloyd Foye** 5tl, 7t, 16/17c, 16t, 17r, 24br, 32/33c, 32t, 33r, 34/35c, 34t, 45tl, 45c, 45r, 62bcl, 62br, 62bcr. **Gino Hasler** 6cr, 12t, 12cr, 13r, 13c, 13bl, 63bl. **Rob Mancini** 5tr, 6br, 7br, 14/15c, 14t, 15c, 15b, 22/23c, 22t, 23b, 23r, 24crt, 25cr, 28/29c, 28t, 29r, 38/39c, 38t, 38b, 39b, 62tl, 62tcl, 62bl, 63tl, 63tcl, 63tr. **Stuart McVicar/Geocart** 8bl. **John Richards** 4br, 42c, 42b, 43cl, 43br, 46/47c, 46t, 48/49c, 48t, 50/51c, 50t, 58/59c, 58t. **P. Scott/Wildlife Art Ltd.** 4crb, 7cb, 20/21c, 20t, 20b, 21b, 24crb, 30t, 30r, 30b, 31b, 31c, 62tr, 63br. **Chris Stead** 43bl, 43cr, 56/57c, 56t, 60/61c, 60t. **Cliff Watt** 45tl, 45c, 45br, 45cr (Maps).
COVER CREDITS
Ad-Libitum FCebl, BCtl (M. Kaniewski). **Jane Beatson** FCcrb. **Dan Cole/Wildlife Art Ltd.** FCl, FCbr, FCtc, BCtr. **Barry Croucher/Wildlife Art Ltd.** FCcrt. **Christer Eriksson** FCc. **Lloyd Foye** Ffc, FCtr, BCb. **Rob Mancini** FCtl, FCebcr, Ffb, BCcr, BCtc, BCtl, Bft, Bfc, Bfb. **Peter Scott/Wildlife Art Ltd.** FCebcl, FCbc, FCebr, Fft. **Chris Stead** FCbl.

Japanese companies have implemented TPM in stages roughly corresponding to the stages of PM development in Japan between 1950 and 1980 (Table 1-2). The information in Table 1-2 is based on data collected in 1976 and 1979 from 124 plants belonging to the JIPM. In three years, the number of plants actively practicing TPM more than doubled. Now, over 20 percent of these factories practice TPM.

		1976	1979
Stage 1	Breakdown maintenance	12.7%	6.7%
Stage 2	Preventive maintenance	37.3%	28.8%
Stage 3	Productive maintenance	39.4%	41.7%
Stage 4	TPM	10.6%	22.8%

Table 1-2. Four Stages of PM Development and the Current Situation in Japan

TPM and the Future of Maintenance

Until the 1970s, PM in Japan consisted mainly of preventive, or time-based maintenance, featuring periodic servicing and overhaul. During the 1980s preventive maintenance is rapidly being replaced by predictive, or condition-based maintenance. The success of TPM depends on our ability to be continuously aware of the condition of equipment in order to predict (and prevent) failures. Predictive maintenance plays a significant role in TPM, because it uses modern monitoring techniques to diagnose the condition of equipment during operation by identifying signs of deterioration or imminent failure.

HOW DOES TPM WORK?

TPM is productive maintenance carried out by all employees through small group activities. Like TQC, which is companywide total quality control, TPM is equipment maintenance performed on a companywide basis. The term TPM was defined in 1971 by the Japan Institute of Plant Engineers (forerunner of

Japan Institute for Plant Maintenance) to include the following five goals:

1. Maximize equipment effectiveness (improve overall efficiency).
2. Develop a system of productive maintenance for the life of the equipment.
3. Involve all departments that plan, design, use, or maintain equipment in implementing TPM (engineering and design, production, and maintenance).
4. Actively involve all employees — from top management to shop-floor workers.
5. Promote TPM through *motivation management*: autonomous small group activities.

The word "total" in "total productive maintenance" has three meanings related to three important features of TPM:

- *Total effectiveness*: pursuit of economic efficiency or profitability
- *Total PM*: maintenance prevention and activity to improve maintainability as well as preventive maintenance
- *Total participation*: autonomous maintenance by operators and small group activities in every department and at every level

The first concept, *total effectiveness* (or "profitable PM"), is emphasized in predictive and productive maintenance (Figure 1-2).

The second concept, *total PM*, was also introduced during the productive maintenance era. It means establishing a maintenance plan for the entire life of the equipment and includes maintenance prevention (MP: maintenance-free design), which is pursued during the equipment design stages. Once equipment is installed, a total maintenance system requires preventive maintenance (PM: preventive medicine for equipment) and maintainability improvement (MI: repairing or modifying equipment to prevent breakdowns and facilitate ease of maintenance).

The last concept, *total participation*, which includes autonomous maintenance by operators and small group activities, is unique to TPM.

	TPM features	Productive Maintenance features	Preventive Maintenance features
Economic efficiency (profitable PM)	O	O	O
Total system (MP-PM-MI)*	O	O	
Autonomous maintenance by operators (small group activities)	O		

TPM = Productive Maintenance + small-group activities

*MP = maintenance prevention
PM = preventive maintenance
MI = maintainability improvement

Figure 1-2. Relationship Between TPM, Productive Maintenance, and Preventive Maintenance

Examples of TPM Effectiveness

TPM has a double goal — zero breakdowns and zero defects. When breakdowns and defects are eliminated, equipment operation rates improve, costs are reduced, inventory can be minimized, and as a consequence, labor productivity increases. As Table 1-3 illustrates, one firm reduced the number of breakdowns to 1/50 of the original number; some companies show 17 to 26 percent increases in equipment operation rates, while others show a 90 percent reduction in process defects; labor productivity generally increased by 40 to 50 percent.

Of course, such results cannot be achieved overnight. Typically, three years are required from the introduction of TPM to achieve prizewinning results. Furthermore, in the early stages of TPM, the company must bear the additional expense of restoring equipment to its proper condition and educating personnel about the equipment. The actual cost depends on the initial quality of the equipment and the technical expertise and experience of maintenance staff. As productivity increases, however, these costs are quickly recouped. This is why TPM is often referred to as "profitable PM."

Category	Examples of TPM Effectiveness
P **(Productivity)**	• Labor productivity increased: 140% (Company M) 150% (Company F) • Value added per person increased: 147% (Company A) 117% (Company AS) • Rate of operation increased: 17% (68% → 85%) (Company T) • Breakdowns reduced: 98% (1,000 → 20 cases/mo.) (Company TK)
Q **(Quality)**	• Defects in process reduced: 90% (1.0% → 0.1%) (Company MS) • Defects reduced: 70% (0.23% → 0.08%) (Company T) • Claims from clients reduced: 50% (Company MS) 50% (Company F) 25% (Company NZ)
C **(Cost)**	• Reduction in manpower: 30% (Company TS) 30% (Company C) • Reduction in maintenance costs: 15% (Company TK) 30% (Company F) 30% (Company NZ) • Energy conserved: 30% (Company C)
D **(Delivery)**	• Stock reduced (by days): 50% (11 days → 5 days) (Company T) • Inventory turnover increased: 200% (3 → 6 times/mo.) (Company C)
S **(Safety/** **Environment)**	• Zero accidents (Company M) • Zero pollution (every company)
M **(Morale)**	• Increase in improvement ideas submitted: 230% increase (36.8/person → 83.6/person) (Company N) • Small group meetings increased: 200% (2 → 4 meetings/mo.) (Company C)

Table 1-3. Examples of TPM Effectiveness (Recipients of the PM Prize)